Pastoral Schools and Colleges

With specific references to health education and drugs, alcohol and smoking

Kenneth David

County Adviser for Schools, Lancashire, with special responsibility for Personal Relationships

James Cowley

INSET Section, The Open University, formerly Director of the Teachers' Advisory Council on Alcohol and Drug Education (TACADE)

Edward Arnold

© Kenneth David and James Cowley 1980

First published 1980
by Edward Arnold (Publishers) Ltd.
41 Bedford Square, London WC1B 3DQ

British Library Cataloguing in Publication Data
David, Kenneth
    Pastoral care in schools and colleges.
    1. Health education—Great Britain
    2. Personnel service in education—Great Britain
    I. Title   II. Cowley, James
    613'.07'1041   RA440.3.G7

ISBN 0-7131-0476-7

Text set in 10/11 pt Linotron 202 Bembo, printed and bound in Great Britain at The Pitman Press, Bath

Foreword by A. J. Collier, M.A., Chief Education Officer, Lancashire

TACADE is a small but vigorous national organisation concerned with alcohol and drug education, and increasingly now with a wider view of health education. The full-time staff led by James Cowley, until recently the Director, have established a high reputation for their in-service work with teachers, a major part of their activities. Kenneth David, Lancashire's County Adviser with Special Responsibility for Personal Relationships, acts as Vice-Chairman.

It is a natural and interesting development for Kenneth David and James Cowley, both of whom have a national reputation for their work in their respective fields, to have collaborated in producing the present book. The subject they write about is difficult, even controversial. The views they express are inevitably personal, but I consider that they present a balanced and practical view of this element of education— the pastoral care of pupils and their education in matters of health with particular emphasis on drugs, alcohol and smoking.

Concern for these matters in every school must surely increase the opportunities for achievement by many pupils, in addition to enhancing the vital preparation of young people for adulthood, parenthood and family life.

Positive health is vital in economic as well as personal terms. I commend the book to teachers everywhere, and particularly to those in secondary schools.

Contents

Introduction

Over the last two decades, there has been a growing belief in schools that young people should be helped more with the personal and affective side of life, as well as the cognitive. This belief manifests itself in the growth of health and social education, in education in personal relationships and in the gradual development of better pastoral care and counselling. The role of the school has continued to develop towards an education of the whole person for the type of society that he will meet when, eventually, he leaves school.

A growing number of schools, and there are outstanding examples in Lancashire for instance, are devoting much effort to careful co-ordination of the affective side of the curriculum and the tutorial system. The curriculum and the timetable are integral parts of the pastoral care system, it seems to us, for the choice of knowledge and the administration of the school teach children about what their teachers see as important in life. Teachers are inevitably models and they are very influential in their way, despite their frequent denial of this. It is not only in special discussions on relationships that pupils learn how to cope with society and its problems: they learn also in most subject lessons and in the workings of the dining room and the school clubs. So a co-ordinated approach to what is dealt with in each subject department and what is dealt with in tutorial and group counselling sessions makes for better relationships with pupils and for better preparation for life. It also produces better cognitive learning and general motivation, in our experience.

Teachers have been helped in some education authorities' areas by well-structured training in pastoral care and by carefully planned pastoral structures within schools. In other areas, forms of pastoral care are still in early days. Whatever the situation, however, the pressures and needs of adolescents are seen throughout the country and teachers are attempting to give appropriate help within the framework which exists.

We can accept that some teachers, because of their personality and ability to relate to young people, will be able to deal easily with many of the emotional and social problems with which young people have to battle. Many teachers, however, when faced with young people using drugs, alcohol and tobacco, lack confidence to deal with these apparently medical or legal issues. Tobacco use can be a sensitive subject because pastoral care has to take into account the attitudes which pupils may have towards school rules and legal constraints; alcohol misuse, now receiving a growing amount of publicity, is a topic with which many teachers have not traditionally concerned themselves, and is again, one where legal aspects are involved; and when faced with the use of illicit drugs, most teachers feel that such situations, so different from the everyday ones with which they normally come into contact, are too difficult for them.

There are added complications which can make the teacher, presented with these aspects of a pupil's behaviour, feel out of his depth. When should parents be informed of incidents concerning alcohol and drugs? How can smokers be helped? How can the pastoral teacher select and help those pupils most likely to have problems with alcohol and other drugs in the future? These are a very small sample of the questions raised when we begin to examine the subject of counselling which is linked with drugs, alcohol and tobacco. Further, if we look behind the situations children discuss with us, there may be areas where chemicals feature as one of many contributory factors to the problems they face. In such cases, the chemical aspect is rarely noticed and less often dealt with. The teacher presented with these problems for the first time may be uncertain how the school would wish the situation to be managed. He may be puzzled, for example, as to whether the head teacher should be informed and whether he can guarantee confidentiality. Even experienced pastoral teachers may be uncertain of the best long-term counselling approaches to use in certain aspects of this field.

When we widen these concerns to consider the whole area of health education it seems obvious to many teachers that a co-ordinated approach to health education throughout the curriculum is an investment in educational and economic terms. Smoking, alcohol and drug misuse are topics within this wider field of health education, and are best dealt with in such a setting, and not in isolation. Recognition of the fact that many modern health risks are self-chosen by the victims indicates a need for new consideration of health education as a priority area.

In this book we discuss basic facts and views on counselling and pastoral care in schools and colleges and the way in which health education—with particular attention to smoking, alcohol and drugs—can be linked with such care. It is intended for teachers holding pastoral appointments and for those working as teacher–social workers or teacher–counsellors, as well as for many teachers who, in their academic teaching or in their tutorial role as form teachers, 'counsel' youngsters in the widest sense of the word. It may also be of value for teachers in training, and as a primer in school-based in-service work. There is also relevance for work in sixth form colleges and further education colleges. We have not, however, attempted to deal with details of welfare, first-aid and discipline, nor with the administration and careers aspects of guidance systems.

When we refer in this text to 'counsellor' we have in mind a teacher with a pastoral and counselling commitment, or a teacher whose relationship with pupils or students brings him many confidences: we have also tried to bear in mind, however, teachers who have a tutorial task and whose teaching gives them an influential role with young people. We hope that it will help teachers to feel more confident in dealing with the basic needs in pastoral care and health education. It is essential that we gain the co-operation and concern of the majority of teachers in working with young people to reduce personal and social problems and so to enable learning to take place.

1

Kinds of counsellors

In the junior school, a child is in a comparatively simple setting and relates most of the time to one familiar teacher. On entering secondary school, a new world opens and frequently it is a much more difficult world. The pupil soon learns to be less free in the way he speaks to teachers and even to his fellow pupils. He begins to retreat gradually from the uninhibited ways of the junior school, for he senses the need for a more guarded approach in the larger school with older pupils. Secondary staff and pupils develop pressures of academic work and seem to have less time to stop and talk. Teachers with specialist roles may see hundreds of children in a week, and a pupil may be able to relate in a personal way with very few of the staff. He has to decide which adults are approachable; good schools will make clear to every young person from the first year what guidance and personal help is available—but whether the reality of life in the institution actually encourages the seeking of help is another matter.

Adults often forget what a confusing picture school can present to a youngster; the pastoral system must not only be available to help pupils with personal problems, but it must also be seen clearly by pupils to be available. A young pupil sees a great deal of movement, a great number of large people—often rather alarming-looking people--and realises that an increasing number of choices and decisions have to be made. As he progresses through the school the confusion may lessen, but the choices and decisions required will increase. The school will rightly require the pupil to show some initiative in seeking the help he needs, for this is the pattern of adult life for which he has to be prepared, but all the time the opportunities for personal and group counselling must be presented in a way which makes them easy to comprehend and readily accessible to pupils.

Society is increasingly concerned with the individual, whose expectations and needs are now apparently given importance. At the same time, the pressures of numbers make individual life difficult. This dichotomy brings pressures in schools and colleges. There is increased community concern, expressed through counselling and pastoral schemes, for the well-being of individual pupils; at the same time, the need to make decisions, to be able to compete with others, and to act with independence among the pressures of adult life, provide alternative and competing needs. We want them to stand alone and make up their own minds against the pressures of society; at the same time we want them to be democratic, to accept the wishes of the majority and to be good, co-operative members of groups. So the need for good counselling schemes seems clear, if pupils are to be helped with decisions and stress.

Learning itself cannot take place in isolation from human feelings and frailties, and schools and colleges which presume that students' personal lives are no concern of the teaching situation are likely to build up frustrations among staff and failures among students. To process and digest some of the vast amount of knowledge which is marketed in our competitive education system requires concentration and motivation, and this cannot exist if minds are busy with personal stresses and worries. To reduce such stresses improves the likelihood of success in our teaching.

The word 'counselling' itself needs definition. It seems to us that the essence of personal counselling is the relationship that is created between two people, in which one seeks support and companionship from the other and in which the comfort and interpretations resulting from the relationship will probably be more important than facts and decisive answers.

In schools and colleges there are different levels of counselling, and we wish at times that different words could be used. The simplest form of 'counselling' in schools is the normal teaching skill of amiably relating to young people and listening to what they have to say, and this happens with most teachers in most classrooms on most days, for it may be considered an everyday part of relationships in a good school. This is to de-mystify counselling, and it is necessary to remind the staff of an educational institution that they can help in solving many problems and motivate and encourage pupils by the good personal relationships that are expected from professional teachers. This simple level of counselling develops in group discussions and tutorial work, for many questions and problems may be answered just by listening to others as part of a group.

A young probationary teacher in a large and lively seaside comprehensive school commented in a training group that his early worries over developing good relationships and easier discipline with his demanding third-year form became markedly easier when he was able to help John, a class personality and leader. Noisy and critical in class registration and tutorial time, John had an untreated minor skin complaint and an apparently uncaring home setting. The teacher sensibly observed and listened and was able eventually to talk with the boy individually and advise him on seeking treatment and, later, on youth and sports club activities. A relationship grew and the class as a whole responded much better, providing an excellent example of a basic level of counselling and pastoral care.

A second level of counselling is required, and hopefully the majority of teachers in an institution will sense when problems are not simple and when referral to other colleagues with more experience and training in counselling skills is wise. Teamwork requires an acceptance of different levels of counselling contributions among a staff, and good pastoral management ensures a repertoire of different levels of counselling among colleagues.

An example of this second level of counselling occurred in an urban, aided comprehensive secondary school where heads of departments at a meeting raised discussion on an under-achieving and troublesome group of fourth-year children of good ability. In this well organised school there followed consultations with the form tutors and year head concerned and a deputy head, a forthright and popular figure, co-ordinated information and approaches in dealing with and obtaining better work from the problem group. A youth worker was later involved, and among other aspects of the discussions with the group was the discovery that heavy drinking was one cause of poor work. Two of the boys confirmed that they could spend four or five pounds in an evening on tinned and bottled beer bought in supermarkets and drunk in depressing surroundings in the town. So a number of problems were eventually disclosed and a number of people were involved in a co-ordinated, thoughtful and yet firm approach with the youngsters.

The third level of counselling could be provided for severe problems by trained counsellors among teachers or other professional workers, and this is where the word 'counselling' has its fullest meaning.

An example of this level of pastoral care occurred in a mixed ability form of fifth-year pupils in a boys' secondary modern school. One boy was withdrawn and occasionally violent with his fellows, and truculent and threatening with teachers. His attendance was fair, his standards of work—when he chose to work—varying from fair to good. He had few friends, and his only discovered interest was in horses and riding. His exhausted form teacher, at his wit's end in how to deal with this and other problems in the group, had the good sense to seek information, through a deputy head, from local people and other professional workers. The true problem of this boy lay in his home conditions, with attempted suicide and prostitution in the family, and other professional workers eventually dealt with the boy and the family, for this was largely beyond teachers' competence, other than to 'support' the boy in this school life.

Counselling requires a belief that each human being has ability, with support, to solve his or her own personal problems though greater support and care may be needed for some who appear to find it difficult to cope. The extent to which all adults are able to put this belief into effect with young people is debatable. Are young people able, with minimum aid from adults, to solve their more testing personal problems? We may over-estimate their abilities, though we must always start by expecting them to manage their own problems.

There can be a dichotomy between individual autonomy and group conformity in schools and colleges and this causes a confusion in pastoral work. If we really mean to prepare people to be autonomous individuals, able to make their own decisions and to solve their own problems, it could turn education upside-down and would force us to rethink the role of every teacher. We pay lip service to this creed of individualism, but practical difficulties—the size of the school, pressures of work, the problems of finding time to know young people, the needs of democratic agreement as well as good order and discipline—make us more concerned with conformity and authority, sometimes in contradiction to necessary personal development and freedom. Good schools succeed in developing pupils as individuals, even within the necessary discipline of an institution, but it requires good teachers, skilled leadership, and a properly managed pastoral system.

Who counsels?

Many people are concerned with counselling young people with their personal problems. Apart from teachers, there are careers officers, educational psychologists, social workers, education welfare officers, youth workers, probation officers and, the most important consellors of all, parents. We can add other popular adults who regularly help young people—the school meals' lady, the caretaker, neighbours, doctors, shopkeepers and a great many other adults. If young people like an adult, they may well talk at a personal level with him, whatever his job, and we can quote examples of schools where ancillary staff are accepted as part of the pastoral team, because they are trusted and sought out by the pupils. A certain urban Roman Catholic secondary school of our acquaintance employs a groundsman who has excellent relationships with pupils and is given their friendship and confidences. The school has an excellent pastoral attitude and the groundsman is viewed as a valued member of the pastoral team, contributing usefully to case discussions at times. A slight snag arises at times, of course, when the visiting supervisor of grounds disagrees with the priority of the groundsman's work—pitches or persons, perhaps!

Teachers may put forward the above point and say that counselling pupils with personal problems is unnecessary in a school because so much is done by others. They could be right, if we think of the many mature youngsters who live in caring families and settings, and they could be right with those youngsters who are so obviously in trouble that many specialists are concerned with them. For a large number of normal pupils, however, this 'trust to luck' attitude, this presumption of implicit support, is not enough. Co-operation is essential to avoid having young people who need support slip through the net of care: difficult youngsters tend to get attention, but withdrawn youngsters can be unnoticed, and the majority of 'normal' pupils with 'normal' problems may well be missed at times.

Peter was intelligent, able and successful at school. He was one of those children who are not right at the top, but are in the next large group, and who are obedient and responsive. He had high aspirations built into him by his parents and by the school. In his last few years at school he had to cope with knowing that he would always be slightly lower in achievement than the friends who formed the 'cream', though he admired them and wanted to reach that same position. When Peter went on to university he adjusted quickly and worked in his same steady way. Then he noticed that it was even harder to keep pace with those who were the most able and this constant desire to excel was counter-productive, producing worry and anxiety which affected his work more and more. A series of low grades in his first-part exams gave him a spell of remorse and he began drinking heavily most nights and gradually became less interested in work. Only through the perceptiveness of a university counsellor dealing with him after an extremely heavy drinking session was it revealed that this was one of many symptoms of an underlying dissatisfaction.

It is easy to recognise that Peter may well have been helped to come to terms with his level of ability had his school taken their role more sensibly in helping pupils to achieve academic excellence. Here the school had seen its role in restricted terms of imparting information and had failed to grasp that the most efficient education is one where students are taught increasingly how to learn. This education would help the student to accept the best methods of learning and their own capabilities and limitations in learning. Peter, like many children, never received this corner-stone of preparation for learning, and he suffered as a result.

It could be argued that this was really the role of the parents. If, however, we accept that, whilst parents play the most important part in the support of their children, schools historically have set themselves up as knowing how to educate, we are likely to conclude that pastoral care for all children is essential in facilitating good learning.

Schools and colleges provide an obvious centre for these caring functions with young people. A school or college is the one place where a pupil will spend many years, where we can ensure that opportunities for counselling are properly structured and where other services and agencies can find a convenient meeting point.

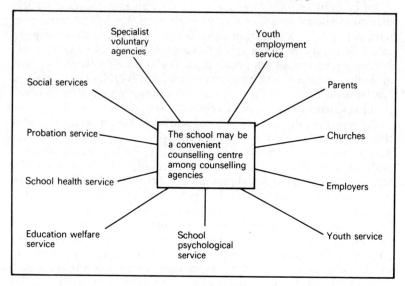

How are pupils influenced?

Pupils like to 'shop around' when they are seeking advice. They may go to a subject teacher they know and trust; they may go to a teacher with a pastoral post; they may reject the school staff and look elsewhere for help and advice. These facts we must accept and a good school will offer itself to the pupils as a guidance community, yet publicise alternative facilities, when they are available, for those who seek them, making sure that a variety of guidance and support is clearly seen. A school staff may decide to intervene when a pupil does not seek advice, but clearly is troubled; if a pupil does not come for help, then help may have to be offered as a part of adult responsibility.

No one person can cope with all the counselling in a school, so there must be a team of teacher-counsellors, based on the work of the many staff who act as form teachers or leaders of tutorial groups. When catching a train one may well question at least two of the railway staff to be sure, and the same concept applies to pupils; they must be able to select from many counselling opportunities. The comprehensive school contains a range of pupils who may vary from an inadequate unskilled worker to the brilliant university teacher of the future. Here is obviously a need for many types of teacher-counsellors, in order that different young people may find the person they need.

To make this facility a reality, there must be ways of demonstrating that teacher-counsellors mean what is said—that they really are helpful people. This is best demonstrated by the counselling staff being well-known to pupils, both from their subject teaching work and from group discussion and tutorial work. Pupils will not obediently flock to be counselled, they are shrewd enough to test the market first.

Teachers can be more influential than they sometimes believe. Young people can be influenced in their career choices and in their academic work by those staff who are sensitive and imaginative and who appear relevant in the personal life of the pupil. The kind of curriculum which is offered can be revealing, and the ways in which subjects are taught can demonstrate the attitudes of staff. Rigidly formal and academic schools do not open much of a personal world for pupils to consider. These may be schools which proudly claim to have no problems—in fact the pupils may have seen that problems are not worth ventilating in the school. The assessment procedures of the school are part of the guidance influence; a constant emphasis on competition and marks lists, on place lists and mock examinations, can make human relationships a fairly distant prospect. The school social system obviously influences the guidance pattern, for the way that groups and activities are arranged must inevitably influence the indications which young people have of whether or not guidance is a personal reality. There are other signs, such as the way parents and visitors are welcomed to the school and the way that the head teacher and staff work together. The quality of attitudes and personalities of the teachers in the school is undoubtedly the most important influence of all. Young people will trust where they see trust and will respond where they see genuineness.

Such influences are more apparent at some times than others. When pupils are about the age of thirteen it is likely that the school will be influential in educational and vocational matters and subject departments may be more important than the pastoral system at this time. The less adequate and problem pupils will perhaps discern most of their clues about the school from the way discipline is administered and from the pastoral system. Pupils who have major problems will see little beyond the attitudes of individual teachers.

What are the requirements for counsellors?

The full-time professional school counsellor should have knowledge of educational tests of all types, be capable of guidance in educational and vocational choices and should have a good knowledge of educational administration. He or she will often be the link with social agencies, a reference and support for colleagues in the school and a link with parents. New pupils in schools will be inducted properly and pupils may well see the professional full-time non-teaching school counsellor as unconnected with authority, perhaps more neutral than the teachers. Many teachers value the full-time school counsellor's role and would argue on these lines.

There are three personal attributes which are valued in both the full-time school counsellor and the teacher-counsellor who is involved with subject teaching and in pastoral and counselling tasks and they are also requirements of most good teachers. The first is the ability to have empathy with others, to be able to 'walk about in another man's skin'. This is different from sympathy, and is something more than imagination and sensitivity. To avoid becoming emotionally in-volved, and yet to have a clear and kindly ability to feel as another person feels is a gift of personality. This is linked with the second attribute, a warmth of manner which is non-possessive and is not paternal. This is not to be confused with a charm of manner which can be switched on and off, but rather is an ill-defined ability to encourage and attract others to a likeable personality trait in the counsellor. This warmth of manner is more easily recognised than described, and we would doubt if it can be developed in training, for it is part of an individual's personality.

The third quality is a genuine interest in people. It is very difficult to accept everyone unreservedly, to accept a young person as he or she is at the time when a problem is presented. A troubled youngster may not be able to explain what he is feeling and may seem obviously to have misunderstood facts and situations. A genuine interest from a teacher, however, means that there is a refusal to criticise and condemn before the expressed feelings are understood. It requires much patience and self-control, because most of us want the young people to be helped to fit into *our* world and to understand the world as *we* see it. A good counsellor may be obliged to move towards a more positive and even directive approach, but should always guard this empathy, warmth and interest —a belief in somebody, even if experience hints that the truth of a problem is quite different from the way it is presented, and even if—as sometimes happens—we are exploited in our concern.

It is essential that those who work with troubled young people have the ability to stand back from their situation and not to become so emotionally involved that they take occasional rudeness or aggres-sion, or apathy and disregard at times, as a personal affront. A teacher-counsellor in a Lancashire school has commented to us that in his work, half his time on subject teaching and half in interviewing and counselling, he seldom expects a tidy ending to a problem or even to know the end at all of many problems. He has also commented wryly that colleagues he has helped with personal problems may avoid him afterwards. Interviewing, by the way, this Lancashire colleague differentiates from counselling. Interviewing to him is when a pupil is sent for to have some matter of behaviour, standards of work, or discipline discussed, often after referral by other staff. Counselling, he claims, is when he has time to talk more relaxedly with a pupil who has sought him out or when an interview situation changes direction to become more of an equal exchange.

Counselling may imply, therefore, gifts of personality which are not necessarily traditional teaching approaches. Counselling may not rest easily with traditional authority, for although the school counselling interview always remains a relationship of an adult with a young person, it is not necessarily a situation where superior and subordinate meet together. True counselling is not imposed, but is rather a partnership in seeking answers and decisions. A pupil should, in theory, be contributing to the counselling by his own choice and in his own right and he can, if he chooses, reject the leads given and the approaches offered. Much personal counselling should be a neutral meeting point and this is why it is difficult for those who have strong views on their status and authoritative position.

Most of us want to solve our own problems, even when we seek the help of others. This applies to young people as well as adults and the counsellor's personality must build up a young person's confidence and, at the same time, enable him to accept responsibility for his own actions. Counselling should enable somebody to work out for himself where his problems or unhappiness may lie. Teachers value the ability to manage their own lives and many will find it difficult to sympathise with those who either cannot manage their own lives or who do not value the ability to do so. The personality and values of the teacher-counsellor are constantly challenged if counselling is done well.

If we can help a person to help himself, we are counselling. This is not a new pursuit or a fresh twentieth-century expertise; people have confided in each other for generations and it is wrong to build up too much mystique about counselling. Of course it is a skill, and of course it is something which is best done by certain types of personality, but it is not a religion nor should it develop too strictly into a learned specialism. If someone is unsuited for counselling then no amount of training will make him into a counsellor. Researchers in America once tried to measure the gains through counselling with psychotic patients. Trained therapists took some groups and young, untrained college students led others. It is an interesting thought that the research claimed that the best gains for patients lay with the groups led by young undergraduates and 'sex, beauty and bounce had the edge!' So counselling is a personality matter, which is not to belittle the need for training and experience. We completely agree with the many kinds of counselling training, but at all times we must recognise that fully trained or even partially trained counsellors will be few in number for many years to come, whilst problems seem to increase.

One of the main arguments in favour of seeking to employ full-time professional school counsellors, as distinct from teacher-counsellors with teaching and guidance commitments, is the difficulty of sustaining two roles: the authority figure and the accepting, neutral counsellor. We consider it is possible for mature teachers to be capable of carrying the two roles, even if it is difficult to discipline pupils and shortly afterwards to be an accepting listener and counsellor for the same pupils. A successful teacher who has a reputation for fairness and who is both confident and quietly firm in his manner should have no difficulty, in our experience. Pupils will go to those they like, even if at other times they have to be disciplined rather than befriended. Those teachers who are known to have major counselling roles may have advantage taken of them, of course, but if such work is limited to experienced and successful teachers, there will not be too much difficulty, provided such teachers are quietly confident and have no major worries about control.

Institutions, and those who serve in them, must have limitations, and inevitably many pupils will have little to do with their teachers; such pupils will seek help elsewhere, for schools cannot be all things to all people. Critics of our viewpoint argue that the conflict of roles is far deeper than we perceive and that children's perception of authority is too deep-rooted for them to accept counselling from teachers in authority; the choice of loyalty to the institution or to the child is too great, they argue, for the traditional teacher to counsel effectively. Whilst not denying the problem, we feel this overstates the problem in practice. The value of trained counsellors who will not appear as authority figures to children is great, but their absence does not preclude confidences from young people.

Pastoral training

Structure and consistency are lacking in the training of teachers in counselling and other aspects of pastoral work in many parts of the country. Some are appointed to a pastoral post solely because they 'have good discipline', seem to be 'sympathetic people' or because they have a good relationship with the other staff; it cannot be ignored also that some appointments to pastoral posts have been made simply to allow the person concerned a promotion to a higher scale. Any new head teacher will therefore have to assess the value of pastoral staff appointed prior to his arrival.

Training may be organised by an education authority, but individual schools may also arrange for their staff to receive training in the institution, looking in detail at certain problems of pastoral care. It is important that training should not consist only of intellectual debate on principles or, at the other extreme, in considering only crisis incidents. Training must aim to help teachers to realise the scope and implications of pastoral care. To give one example, a teacher may be well versed in the signs and facts of illicit drug use amongst children and yet be blind to the fact that a child who is constantly being counselled for depression has a father who is an alcoholic. Training must also bring out the different attitudes which must exist between different members of a pastoral team. Expressing and sharing these attitudes in training enables a head teacher, year tutor or counsellor to know which staff member might be most helpful for a particular child's needs.

In-service training of a school staff together in their own school has many advantages over individuals attending courses elsewhere on their own. When a team trains together, factual knowledge and case studies can be used to develop the growth of the team as a whole and the problems each member is facing can be discussed and support offered. In such circumstances the team's expertise will grow. This is not to decry other forms of centralised training. Pastoral teams may need to meet staff from other schools, and to receive more advanced training than can be offered in the school. An education authority needs to provide central training for pastoral staff for them to become fully effective, but the school also needs to organise its equally valuable local training. Good counselling causes not only the person being counselled but also the counsellor to develop and be tested as an individual, and effective team support should be provided for the teacher-counsellor.

Centralised basic training offered by a local education authority for pastoral staff will probably include a good deal of carefully planned and carefully led group work, discussing a number of main themes of relationships which occur in counselling, and emphasising and examining the teachers' own feelings and attitudes; no one can easily counsel others without carefully considering his own attitudes and prejudices, preferably in a group setting. Counselling skills and methods will also be considered in local education authority short courses, together with discussion techniques. Information will be needed on a number of subjects, including specific themes such as alcohol, drugs and smoking.

A typical training course for senior staff of secondary schools in Lancashire includes the following sessions, spread over six days of residential training, three days in the autumn term and three days in the spring term, with group meetings and set reading in the interval.

(1) Assemble; introduction to course.

(2) Tutor groups—discussion in small groups.

(3) The techniques of discussion work.
(4) Working with groups—a survey of group dynamics.

(5) Tutor groups.
(6) A review of secondary school pastoral systems.
(7) Childhood and adolescence.
(8) The form tutor's role.
(9) Tutor groups.

(10) Counselling and interviewing.
(11) Health education and education in personal relationships (EPR)—the co-ordinator's role.
(12) Tutor groups.

(13) Assemble; introduction to second part of course.
(14) Personal and group counselling.
(15) Specific areas of health education—VD, abortion, contraception, alcohol, drugs, smoking.
(16) Moral education.
(17) Tutor groups.

(18) Co-ordinating a health/social/EPR programme—visiting speakers.
(19) Friendship and loneliness.
(20) Discipline, authority, and aggression.
(21) Tutor groups.
(22) Simulation exercise—winning colleagues' confidence.
(23) Liaison and referral with other agencies—visiting speakers.
(24) The school context—the purpose of education.

Local training for all the staff of a school can usefully concentrate on the role of the form teacher or form tutor, and this will bring consideration of the skills of observation, discussion, interviewing and counselling of a simple nature, as well as clarifying administrative and other duties. Linking this work with the role of the school's appointed pastoral staff in a team approach should illustrate how the school's pastoral system interlocks. It should thus illustrate how counselling and pastoral work is dependent on the combined work of all the staff of a school, in tutorial time and in normal classroom work, as well as in leisure pursuits.

A useful in-service training programme in tutorial work in a Lancashire high school was as follows.
(1) Earlier planning meetings with a representative group of staff.
(2) The preparation and issue of a seminar handbook, containing handouts of all talks and contributions.
(3) Afternoon closure of the school for:

(a) talk to all staff on the form tutor's role;
(b) contributions on their view of tutorial work by a visiting form tutor, pastoral head, deputy head, and an educational welfare officer—These emphasise the tutor's role, the value of supportive material for form discussions, the relevance of family background, and the need for proper referral and liaison;
(c) discussion in groups, the leaders having been previously briefed;
(d) a final session for questions.

(4) Half the school staff are made available on another afternoon, a fortnight later for:
(a) a talk by a curriculum development officer on materials and methods for the tutorial period;
(b) discussion on case studies;
(c) a final question session.

(5) The other half of the staff have a similar session a week later.

(6) Afternoon closure of the school for:
(a) a talk to all staff on 'Observing young people', covering: observation skills, normal and abnormal problems, vulnerable children, stress in relationships, danger signals to note, listening techniques and communication problems between people;
(b) discussion in groups;
(c) talks from a police officer, social service officer, educational psychologist, Samaritan counsellor and a medical officer, on 'Young people under stress';
(d) final question session.

(7) Staff groups prepare comments later on these seminars, and offer advice on school improvements in pastoral work, and on future in-service needs of staff.

2

Kinds of counselling

There are a number of views of counselling, variations in the pattern and opposing views and schools of thought. Much of the controversy about different styles of counselling is artificial, for few who are responsible for counselling follow particular counselling philosophies– –they live with their own personality and varying approaches to counselling all serve their purpose at different times for different people.

There are three main counselling tasks in schools: personal or individual counselling, educational counselling and vocational counselling. Vocational counselling deals with careers advice and education, but the word 'counselling' adds an extra dimension, for it implies that this is a sharing of views about vocations between adults and young people, rather than advice on what a child could do. Vocational guidance in a school or college is sometimes part of the duty of the pastoral team or it may be the work of a separate careers section. Careers counselling needs to be better recognised in our schools in the future, for it has too little attention in many schools at present.

Educational counselling is usually the responsibility of subject departments, though pupils may also need further counselling support apart from this. Educational guidance is generally done well, but the growth in the size and complexity of schools and the variety of choices available to pupils at the age of thirteen make this an increasingly important area. The link with careers counselling is obvious. The choice of subjects and examinations that the pupil makes is linked with the kind of career that he desires and the expectations of life style that he has been encouraged to hold by home and school. Those who offer educational guidance may base their advice on a simple assessment of the pupil's present standards or they may take a longer view of the potential of a child, with less emphasis on marks and class placings.

Personal counselling deals with an individual pupil's questions, problems, situations, excitements and doubts. In schools and colleges it is normally an informal relationship between an adult and a young person, discussing particular problems and situations. Counselling can deal with 'pathological' or 'normal' cases. We feel that counselling is largely a normal process that most people can accept as part of their education, dealing with natural developmental problems. It is about the way that normal problems and crises are dealt with for most of the pupils in the school, whether in groups or as individuals. To others, counselling is seen as a department of lost causes, dealing with the abnormal, the unusual and the difficult. The answer probably lies with both views; counselling is concerned with normality and with temporary problems, but equally it is deeply concerned with the passengers and the inadequates in life. It is sometimes argued that too deep a concern with the abnormal and the inadequate can create 'clinical careers'—an over-concern which separates troubled young people from normal settings, always isolating them as a problem. This can happen, for concern can lead to the kind of counselling attention which processes a youngster into a problem career in the school. This is often the case with difficult and aggressive pupils, but less frequently so with those who are withdrawn and inadequate. One way of resolving this is for a few skilled teacher-counsellors on a staff to give particular attention to those who need much time and attention, but with the majority of the staff dealing with normal problems and crises, often in tutorials and group discussions. There is also a danger of the remedial departments in secondary schools becoming the repository of those who do not fit elsewhere and therefore becoming an enclave of problem pupils. It must be better to withdraw such pupils from their regular classes for remedial work, with the pupil returning to 'normal' groups and companions for many other activities and subjects.

We speak of individual and group counselling. Individual counselling is self-explanatory—the individual talks with a counsellor, or even a pair of counsellors, if this is the best way of dealing with the situation. Group counselling may consist of several pupils being guided and counselled in a group, where they have similar problems. Such group counselling is often done with from two to perhaps five or six young people and with a particular problem in mind; perhaps a group which is causing disciplinary troubles or a group which is at risk in some way—drinking for example, or shop-lifting, or apparent promiscuity

A sixth form group had gradually developed as a group because of their common interest in motorcycles. One of the boys had become interested in the phenomenon of 'chapters'—organised groups of motorcycle riders deriving a common identity from their activities. They found, however, considerably difficulty in having a place to meet. At the youth centre, they were viewed with suspicion because of their bikes, their clothes and the image they displayed. At the local pubs, the landlords tried to move them on because they didn't help custom—people always seemed to fear that trouble might occur.

They found, however, that the only places they could meet were the pubs, but increasingly as the group developed they precipitated various troubles through drinking and through minor incidents of violence.

A teacher developed a good relationship with the group and was able to see behind the drink/driving offences and the violence, which might well have been the only things taken up and dealt with. Instead, because of his perceptiveness, he recognised that they wanted identity and needed a meeting place and many of their problems were symptoms of being unable to find somewhere satisfactory. By helping them to arrange a more suitable clubroom, he was able to build up his relationship with the group and slowly be drawn into a position where they felt free to 'bounce' their thoughts off him, and use him as an aid in the way they functioned as a group in helping each other.

There is a distinction between crisis and continuous counselling. Counselling should be a normal and continuous process during a young person's time at school or college, instead of offering help only when crises arise. It is far better if, by various procedures, young people have the opportunity to ventilate problems and reduce pressures before crises develop. This is sometimes referred to as the difference between the event and the process: 'events' bring situations, temporary or lasting, which have to be dealt with as a single occasion in counselling, often with some element of urgency. 'Process' indicates a long-term view of a problem with the origins and build-up of that problem being discerned and eased before it becomes a crisis. The whole of the pastoral and academic work of a school should be leading the pupils towards a positive and healthy approach to life and the concept of 'continuous counselling' supports such aims. Yet crises will still occur, for life is never tidy, and a good school will have to be capable of dealing with both event and process counselling.

A pastoral crisis that occured in one school, which had a first class tutorial and pastoral system, was concerned with drink. A group of youngsters bought brandy in a supermarket one lunch time and decided to return to school in a lively mood. Disruption of afternoon lessons followed, and later came scenes of remorse with hangover headaches, sickness and protestations of 'never intending to touch another drop'. All this was dealt with expertly and quietly, and the staff argued that it was a measure of trust that the group did return to school in the afternoon! It is interesting, however, to note that the drinking crisis occurred despite a useful health education programme in the school, carefully co-ordinated and teaching pupils how to live with alcohol. Perhaps we have to expect experimentation as inevitable and be geared to cope with it, for the young never have heeded all the warnings of their elders.

Directive and non-directive counselling

There is a distinction between directive and non-directive counselling.

At the one extreme is the 'client-centred therapy' of Carl Rogers, in which counselling is seen as a reflective process with the counsellor acting as a mirror to the client. At the other extreme could be behavioural counselling, in which the counsellor accepts responsibility for teaching a client the skills he needs and actively remedies the deficits in the client's understanding and experience. There is a world of a difference between advising and directing in a very positive way and accepting and reflecting in a completely neutral way. Most good counselling is probably based on an eclectic approach, but we can consider the extreme positions for a while.

To be very positive and directive in dealing with somebody's problems might be very 'British'. In Britain we have believed in the past in firm leadership for those in trouble, in an unquestioning faith in the sound judgement of authority and in a caring and paternal belief in directing the welfare of others. At this extreme, counsellor-centred guidance can simply be advice-giving. If somebody wants to know a fact, it is probable that he will be told what he wants to know. There are many jokes about the person who asks a straighforward question requiring a straightforward answer being given instead an interview he does not seek.

'Sir, where's the office?'
'Ah, come on in and sit down lad, and we'll discuss your problem.'

Good counsellors will clearly give advice on many occasions. They cannot be other than positive and factual if they are asked for straightforward opinions on things verifiable by facts.

There is a wider field of counselling in which there is a great temptation to give advice when it may, in fact, be quite wrong. This arises when facts are questionable and when attitudes and values are involved. It is difficult to believe though, that a teacher with a very positive and directive personality will seek to lay down the law when it is a matter of choice of values. Common sense must dictate that to be too directive is often to lose the trust of the person being counselled, which, by the way, does not mean that we cannot remain positive people.

If a student reveals to a teacher that he has smoked 'pot' once or twice, it is easy for some to respond only by attempting to persuade the young person not to continue because it is against the law and the school's accepted norms and will lead to the student being seen as a deviant. However, we may then be so directive that we alienate the young person whose real problem is how to handle the social situation, where the norm is to smoke 'pot', rather than the 'pot' smoking itself.

Directive counselling is an intellectual approach in which the counsellor presumes his better knowledge and understanding, demanding facts and decisions from the client, then accepting responsibility for interpreting the problems and guiding the client. This is god-like, for it presumes that the counsellor, because of his training, maturity and intellect, is better able to decide the answer than the person who has the problem. It is unlikely that a very directive counsellor would attempt to offer answers until he has listened and balanced and questioned, but to be directive is very tempting, especially for teachers who are short of time and who work in authoritative settings, where young people are seldom viewed as being responsible.

It is argued that such counsellor-centred guidance suits certain clients, especially those who seek a factual response, and perhaps it is more often present when counselling young people, especially those who are inadequate or inarticulate. No counselling, however, can safely be presumed to require this kind of directive approach without thought and preparation by discussion and careful listening. Problems can sometimes be 'presenting' problems, covering a deeper question or need—there can be 'music behind the words'. How can we with certainty know that the solution which seems so clear to the counsellor is suitable for the person seeking aid? Directive counselling clumsily used can make a young person responsive for a while, but resentful in the long term, can produce greater dependence and inferiority, and can reduce rather than improve personal confidence.

Client-centred counselling

If we establish the person being counselled as the central figure in the counselling relationship, relegating the teacher-counsellor to a non-directive receiving role at the beginning of the interview, we have a totally different viewpoint. If a counsellor regards the counselling interview as a model of a relationship, then he may see the value of avoiding advice-giving and directive approaches. Each counselling interview is, in fact, an example for the young person of the way that two people can relate to each other in a friendly and caring way and this is impossible if the counsellor is at all authoritative or too demanding in the partnership.

Every person, even the most awkward and difficult, has some worth and dignity. A non-directive counsellor is a receiving person, able through empathy to absorb the feelings and words and problems of another, regarding him as equally human. This requires a considerable strength of personality in the counsellor and a great belief in the worth of others. It implies that most people have the ability within themselves to comprehend their own problems; it presumes that the answers to problems will probably lie within the mind of the person in the problem situation and it implies a trust in the human potential to be self-motivating. The Quakers say, 'There is that of God in every man': this perhaps indicates the approach of the truly non-directional counsellor.

This need not imply that the non-directive counsellor is a negative person, a counselling wallpaper. Although the counsellor may appear to ask little, seek little and demand nothing, he will be positive in seeking to help the young person to comprehend his problem and understand his feelings, in ways which do not reduce a person's confidence or threaten his view of himself. A non-directive counsellor still asks questions, comments and suggests, but at all times does so from a position of equality.

In a memorable section of one of his books, Carl Rogers* sums up the philosophy of client centred counselling:

If I can create a relationship characterised on my part:

by a *genuineness and transparency*, in which I *am* my real feelings;
by a *warm acceptance* and prizing of the other person as a separate individual;
by a sensitive ability to see *his world and himself* as he sees them;

Then the other person in the relationship:

will experience and understand aspects of himself which previously he has repressed;
will find himself becoming better integrated, more able to function effectively;
will become more similar to the person he would like to be;
will be more self-directing and self-confident;
will become more of a person, more unique and more self-expressive;
will be more understanding, more acceptant of others;
will be able to cope with the problems of life more adequately and more comfortably.

The co-operative approach

It is said that between *laissez-faire* and indoctrination lies the art of nurturing. This seems to us to sum up the concept of a co-operative and eclectic approach to counselling. This is the common-sense view that many people will find both natural and particularly helpful with young people. It should give the best of both approaches and it is particularly necessary when a young person has sought us out, rather than our sending for him.

The counsellor and the young person are both equal, both contributing their own points of view to the problem and both contributing

* Rogers, C., *On Becoming a Person,* Constable, 1971.

to the facts, conditions and relationships which must be seen before the person can try to find his own solution. The counsellor contributes in a 'give and take' way, never dominating or indoctrinating, but avoiding being negative. Ultimately, it is the young person who must choose the action, solution or acceptance of the problem. The co-operative approach contributes to this positively, but avoids being directive in an absolute way, nor is it totally accepting in a non-directive way.

The counsellor recognises, of course, that every individual has to take the responsibility for his or her own life, and if the counsellor is a normal and busy person, he has neither the time nor the wish to try to accept total responsibility for the life of another. He knows that a co-operative and free approach means an equal participation in making decisions about a problem, never leaving the person feeling he is unimportant or negative. This mutual type of approach implies a respect for differences, but a natural way of contributing—neither distancing oneself from the person, nor dominating him. The good counsellor will vary his manner, and will be considering all the time the effect of his own intervention on the young person and on his background and friends and parents.

It is helpful to think of this co-operative approach as having a cycle of method by the counsellor, and we have been greatly influenced by Douglas Hamblin in the model outlined below.*

Most of us would instinctively be quite non-directive, unquestioning and receptive when first considering a problem with a client. This hardly needs saying, for a counsellor who is too quick to intervene, too brisk with his questions or conceited enough to jump to quick conclusions cannot really be very helpful. A difficulty may arise when a person is shy, nervous and inarticulate; a relaxed and reflective conversation about the background of the person may help to set him at ease and perhaps help him find words. We must not be afraid of silence, however, for if the counsellor's manner and appearance is relaxed and welcoming, then words will eventually come.

As the situation is opened up we listen, sometimes listening to evident misrepresentations of situations and facts, but constantly listening and accepting. Even misunderstandings and false assumptions are real in their consequences and therefore are real to a person if he is emotionally concerned. Gradually, however, a counsellor begins to interpret, to offer his own instinctive reactions to statements made and, occasionally, in a manner of equal participation, will intervene with facts and arguments. This is the stage of a counselling interview when there should be true equality and when a co-operative approach really has meaning. The non-directive opening can quite naturally

* Hamblin, D., *The Teacher and Counselling*, Blackwell, 1974.

lead to this kind of equal dialogue, though the counsellor must still do far more listening than talking. Gradually the client should be helped to identify certain goals, and certain facts about his problem or situation, and it is then likely that, with young people, the counsellor may move to a more positive role as time goes on. If there has been a genuine and leisured assessment of the situation and if the counsellor has with absolute honesty helped the student to suggest what may be the action to take, or the attitude to accept, then it is quite reasonable and honest to begin to direct him towards certain action. This is where directive counselling can be acceptable. Not everyone who comes to a counsellor is able to assume full responsibility for themselves, nor does self-understanding and analysis come easily to all people. A good counsellor may quite naturally move from reception and exploration of the problem towards persuasion that the student shall actually do what has been mutually discerned as reasonable and positive action. In the case of young people, it is often necessary to provide support and resources, so that what the young person has seen as the right action can actually take place. So we move from being supportive to being positive, from reflection to action, from being non-directive to being directive.

If we take the earlier example slightly further, we have the young student smoking 'pot' occasionally. Instead of starting directively we would need to start by being supportive and positive. To do this would not mean necessarily condoning the action, but exploring more fully the social and other reasons for the behaviour and the feelings of the young person. This would slowly develop into positively drawing out from the student whether there were changes he or she wanted to make in handling the social situation and how they could go about it. The discussion would move from reflection on what has occurred to working out strategies for handling similar situations in the future. The counsellor could move from non-directively accepting how the student felt and behaved to more positive directive help in forcing the student to weigh up the consequences of alternative actions he could take, rather than just seeing one course of action.

Sustaining techniques

In good counselling, the ability to listen is vital and a receptive attitude is essential in most counselling interviews. We show interested, sympathetic listening by the way we speak, look and sit. Without being too studied or artificial, it is necessary to look relaxed and interested. We should attempt to indicate acceptance, and have about us an appearance of calm and relaxation. This can be independent of our personal feelings; we may not like an individual, but we can still have an absolute belief in his value and we can demonstrate this in the way we react to him. So we must sustain and relax those who come to us for counselling by our manner, by the setting and environment and, most important of all, by our genuine belief that others are important.

So we talk and consider, suppose and explain, discuss and argue, and are sometimes silent with out client. We share and discuss a problem or a situation between two people or within a group, mostly in a quiet and reflective way—we 'ventilate' a problem. Sometimes, however, strong feelings are released and a troubled person or an angry group will pour out their feelings in words and emotions. This can be a proper relief for tension and sometimes it is inevitable, but at the same time it can be unfortunate, because such an outburst may bring an exposure of someone's inner self or a loss of dignity and this may not be the right thing for a particular counselling interview. A counsellor must judge when such an outburst should be diverted and when it is right to bear with an outburst of emotion. A sensitive counsellor can sense when emotions are near boiling point and, if it seems inappropriate, he can change the atmosphere and direction of the interview to give a client time to cool down. One can sometimes lose the opportunity for other counselling interviews if a breakdown brings embarrassment and a vague feeling of shame. A young person may then avoid further contact.

The writer recalls an incident in which a student who had attempted suicide had many, many hours of counselling and, with the help of a supportive family, was helped back to a balanced view of life and study. Yet, weeks later, the youngster crossed a street near the college to avoid contact, for the counsellor was presumably associated with an episode to be firmly put into the past. Hurtful at the time, the action had to be seen as a not unnatural consequence of the counselling story.

A counsellor endeavours to divide up problems and situations so that they are comprehensible to the student. A problem that is considered as a series of parts may be more easily understood than an overwhelming whole. A counsellor may also recall the rule of parsimony: teachers and lecturers may tend to labour a point, but in counselling as in teaching, once is often enough and repetition can spoil the effect. Providing we think that a point has got home, it is often best to leave it at that, rather than constantly to reiterate it because we are worried lest it has not been fully appreciated.

Development through counselling

If we accept that, apart from listening, we are also helping the person being counselled towards his own solutions and actions—nurturing him—we will see counselling as a process which helps people to develop. Everyone faces problems at some stage or another and a counsellor would normally not only be considering the immediate situation, but will always be considering it as part of the long-term development of the individual. The counsellor has to envisage the student as he can be in the future or as he has been in the past, rather than only seeing him at the moment of crisis. In this way we use a particular piece of counselling as a point in growth, rather than as an effective piece of first aid.

This means that a counsellor will be aware of the possibility of future problems, as well as immediate problems, and this may require an ability to discern excessive stress, which will require referral to a specialist counsellor. Specialists must deal with severe stress problems, and thus we must attempt to see a whole person as he has been and will be, rather than just the troubled person before us at the time of counselling.

We must also accept that saying 'no' can be a very positive way of caring and an over-sentimental or too liberal approach may be wrong. Again, we see in a co-operative and developmental approach to counselling that we can be directive at times, but only if we are aware of our obligations to keep such directive counselling in perspective.

Developmental counselling may also imply a team approach to counselling in an institution. Counselling is not only a one-to-one relationship; sometimes we can share counselling with other adults who know and care for the individual, and we may wish to avoid any tendency to over-emphasise the need for a troubled person to be dealt with by one selected counsellor on the staff of a school. Many troubled youngsters will be talking to several adults, often at the same time and often without the others knowing. A team approach in school counselling will obviously mean a sharing of responsibilities amongst a staff team. A young person may go to one of a team or may go elsewhere when he is seeking help and advice. If all members of the staff of such teams work well together and have sympathy and trust each other's work, there is no feeling of competition as to which pupil goes to whom. Our aim is to offer a repertoire of counselling to any pupil or any group of pupils and what matters finally is the quality of relationship that best helps an individual pupil. Hence, we will offer facilities for individual counselling, with a number of different personalities available to be approached; and we will also, as a matter of vital concern, offer various kinds of counselling through groups.

As part of this developmental concept, we should keep trying to avoid too great a gap between school and home. Every time we talk with students, we are talking for their parents as well and we must avoid any feelings of superiority in our professional competence and any feeling that it is always the home which is the cause of all the troubles we face in schools. We must avoid stereotyping young people according to our knowledge of their background. Again a good team approach and a wide view of counselling will avoid the dangers of labelling. This is particularly the case with aggressive and troublesome students, but it can also come from a narrow school view, as though the young person only has reality during school hours. 'That illegitimate, adopted West Indian girl' could describe a piece of stereotyping. Every pupil is a person in his own right, with a greatly varied background of influences and attitudes, and a school is only one segment of a young person's life; so, as we see a troubled young person, we also try to glimpse their hidden world away from us, in order that we may relate it to their present problem and to their future development.

It is essential for an effective counsellor always to be assessing what the background and environment of the client are, for nobody lives in isolation from their setting. As we reflect with a student and mutually decide on possible action and assessment of feelings, we should always be offering through our contributions a reminder of what will happen when the interview is ended and the client is back in his normal setting. As we receive facts, information, attitudes and feelings, so we assess how our co-operative ideas will work in other places. It is easy enough to talk about possible actions during a personal and involved dialogue between two people, but the counsellor partner must also be considering the effect elsewhere. A pupil or student can be helped towards some possible action, but that action will produce further effects on fellow pupils in a school, on staff in a school, on friends and on parents. Troubled people can be obsessed with themselves and a counsellor reminds them that counselling affects others.

A summary of simple methods

(1) We must be honestly interested, a concerned and genuine listener. Teachers sometimes feel some pride in their ability to act a part; this is not what counselling needs.

(2) We must listen without interruption and in a setting which gives some privacy. Silences are necessary in counselling, and gentle reflective questions. The counsellor's 'companionable grunt' can ease the business of talking. A major fault of most human beings is that they are too busy to listen properly because they are thinking of what to say next.

(3) There should be plently of time, which raises obvious organisational problems in schools. It is hardly fair to rush a troubled person, but where does the balance of priorities lie—with a restless waiting class or an anxious individual? This is where a full time counsellor can be invaluable, of course, though it is often possible to arrange timetable cover for teachers with counselling commitments.

(4) Some kind of neutral ground is ideal, to provide an easy opportunity for young persons to truly relax and unburden themselves of their problems. Where neutral ground can lie in an institution is difficult to say, but some attempt to provide a peaceful enclave should be attempted.

(5) It is not our job to condemn, but it is equally not our job to condone. If we are genuine in our counselling endeavours, we should not express shock or allocate blame. At the time of counselling, we must accept a troubled person as they are at that moment.

(6) Everyone's problem is unique to himself and we must take people seriously. Other peoples' problems are sometimes funny, though ours are never so, and the counsellor who breezily makes light of another's misfortunes may be indicating that he is afraid to think very deeply about it. This is not to suggest that every counselling interview is a solemn affair, for laughter may well be part of it. There is a difference between the way that an adult appears to a young person to be superior in his laughter or ridicule and that adult's own impression of himself as being able to laugh the young person away from his problem. On the whole, a serious note must predominate as we listen to others. Our own sensitive judgement should tell us when the time is right to reduce a problem to size with a joke or laughter.

(7) An important task of a counsellor is to put other points of view. It is easy enough to offend someone who is absorbed in their own point of view of their problem by giving a contrary viewpoint, but this is the truth of a truly co-operative approach. We are often the spokesman for others when talking with a young person and, if our manner is genuine and acceptable, this is part of being in a shared counselling situation.

(8) Few problems have tidy endings and solutions may often be impossible. Our sense of tidiness seldom likes this, and we may attempt to have a decisive ending. A clear ending may be possible if the student sees a solution—in this shared thinking we will obviously offer a number of suitable alternatives for the youngster to consider—but we must accept that in the end we may only be able to support, listen and reflect. It is often our fate never to know the end of the story and some stories cannot have an ending.

(9) We must see behind the story. A 'presenting' problem may be what the young person wishes to open the conversation with, but the true question may well be something different. Without labouring this, we must be strongly aware of the fact that many problems lie under layers of other situations. We must be sure what somebody is unhappy about and until we are sure our opinions and advice are highly debatable.

3

Pastoral systems and tutorial work

The pastoral system

The aims of school pastoral work have been suggested as follows.*
(1) (a) To create a sense of order and purpose with opportunities for diagnosis and possibilities for change;
(b) to recognise, assess and develop individual potential as a necessary preparation for sound educational and vocational guidance and teaching;
(c) to gain some knowledge of the pupil's home background and its influence on the pupil's development and progress;
(d) to know something of the pupil's personal problems;
(e) to offer guidance and counselling, so helping young people to make their own decisions;
(f) to assist individuals to develop their own life-styles and to respect those of others.

(2) 'Pastoral care is an expression of the school's continuing concern for the individual's integrity and welfare, its involvement in the development of his personality and talents, and its readiness to support him at all times and especially when his work is adversely affected by personal or domestic circumstances.' (P. Smart, H.M.I.)

From this we see that the purpose of pastoral work in secondary schools is to facilitate learning and to help pupils in their personal development. Since these are also the aims of many academic departments, the question can reasonably be raised, 'Why so much concern about pastoral work?'

The most obvious reason is that family and community life become more complex as modern society develops, and teaching and learning must be affected by this. We know schools with over half the children from broken or disturbed families and it takes little investigation to find that the troubled or demanding personal background of pupils affects their schooling. If we ignore or limit the welfare and social

* Acknowledgment is made for material from several sources, including Northumberland Park School, Tottenham.

responsibilities of a school, we are likely to have an inefficient place in which to learn.

Pressures on teachers increase, and to presume that all the staff of a school are observant, sensitive and caring and that they have time to deal with pastoral care in normal class teaching, is optimistic. While the majority of pastoral care does belong with the general work of the staff, we cannot rely upon this as the only answer. Specialist staff and careful planning and training are essential additions. Just as specialist English teachers support and lead their colleagues in the school's contribution to English work, so selected and efficient pastoral heads can advise and support teachers in their vital tutorial role, in counselling matters and in co-ordinating welfare, health and social education; and with this should go careful management. Some of the best schools we know appear to have a relaxed and flexible system of pastoral management, but invariably there has been intensive and imaginative planning of both teaching and tutorial care, and the form tutor forms the essential basis of the pastoral system.

In this planning the following selection of questions may be starting points.

(1) Are the school's aims and objectives clear to all staff?

(2) Are pupils' records informative, accurate and available?

(3) How are everyday administrative tasks arranged—to be efficient but brisk? How are general announcements made?

(4) How is information on pupils shared between teachers?

(5) Is there general agreement on how confidential matters and pupils' confidences are to be treated? How is the head teacher to be kept informed?

(6) Are welfare and medical arrangements fully understood and used?

(7) Are free school meals organised in a kindly way? Are the educational welfare officer and school nurse members of the pastoral team? How should the office staff help?

(8) What arrangements exist for close liaison with voluntary and statutory agencies?

(9) Is careers education practical and helpful?

(10) Is educational guidance helpful and thorough?

(11) Are all children known well by several teachers?

(12) Are slow learners and gifted children identified?

(13) Are parents notified of what the school does and are they helped to feel involved in a co-operative approach to the personal and learning problems of pupils?

(14) Does the timetable help the tutorial system? How much time do form tutors have with their groups?

(15) How are the tutorial groups organised and is change in membership possible?

(16) How does the school encourage the pupils' social competence?

(17) In tutorial work: How are questions on controversial matters dealt with? What curriculum materials are helpful to aid discussions? Is there an L.E.A. policy on education in personal relationships or health education? Can visitors and experts help at times? Is there general agreement, or at least frank discussion, between staff on general moral issues?
(18) Are all teachers potential form tutors? Should some be exempted or excluded from this role?
(19) How does a tutor 'get to know' the pupils in his/her form, and how can the school help this by organisation?
(20) How does a tutor discover potential and develop talents?
(21) How can pastoral care constantly be linked with subject teaching?
(22) What are the limits of pastoral care, and when might it become intrusive and unnecessary?

The pastoral head

Many schools have year or house heads, the most common kind of pastoral appointment, and increasingly we have posts as head of Lower, Middle and Upper School. Other exotic terms are used in schools, such as 'linesmen', 'sentinels' and 'section chairman'. The following is a selection of items from job specifications of such pastoral heads.

In addition to his normal subject teaching, which should have some priority, the duties of a year or house head *may* include all or some of the following.
(1) Ensuring that his or her team of form tutors meet regularly and understand the policy of the school on all important matters, and develop their groups so that every child feels the school is doing everything possible to develop his or her social and academic capabilities to the fullest extent.
(2) Co-ordinating all information received from and given to year heads and form tutors, and checking that action is taken when necessary.
(3) Encouraging and co-operating with form tutors with regard to the general welfare of the children, and mutually to develop good discipline.
(4) Representing the views of form tutors in discussions with other senior staff, and informing the head teacher of the development of the year group.
(5) Co-ordinating supervisory responsibilities of staff and monitors/prefects.
(6) Knowing pupils in the year as well as possible and trying to become accepted as a person to whom they can turn for guidance.

(7) Having a watching brief over the academic progress of pupils in the year, taking action when necessary, in conjunction with other colleagues.

(8) Co-ordinating the keeping of written records of individual children, ensuring that record cards are kept up to date, perhaps with key symbols to represent certain problems.

(9) Providing (in conjunction with the form teachers) pupils' school reports, and confidential reports or references when required.

(10) Checking attendance registers, ensuring with the form tutor's help that reasons for absence, truancy and unpunctuality are checked.

(11) Arranging meetings with parents or writing to parents in order to acquaint them with school policy, or discussing the welfare and general problems arising with any particular child, occasionally visiting children's homes either at the wish of the school or a request from the parents.

(12) Liaising closely with other services such as: social services, educational welfare officer, police liaison officer and medical staff.

(13) Preparing morning assembly.

(14) Taking responsibility for lunchtime arrangements and duties if required, granting permission for children to go out of school where necessary.

(15) Liaising with others in organising careers guidance, and organising with colleagues the tutorial work, and social and extra-curricular functions.

(16) Organising representatives from each form to make up a year council. Chairing and convening regular meetings of the year council and putting forward their views as appropriate.

(17) Co-operating with staff responsible for liaising with other schools in order to ensure the smooth transfer of children.

(18) Meeting regularly with other year tutors, and assisting in staff in-service training.

It was recently put very forcibly by an overworked year head, that successfully to carry out all this job specification would merit instant promotion to head teacher! The posts are important and demanding and can affect the work of the school profoundly. One of the worst staffing errors a head teacher can make is to appoint lesser quality teachers to such posts, as a professional side track.

The form tutor

The central pastoral value of the school has to be the good class teacher and form tutor, well prepared and well supported. Observant, caring teachers, each with their subject commitment, are our chief investment.

Since there are only limited opportunities for individual counselling and interviewing in a busy school we should look to group work by the class tutor as a vital form of preventive counselling. As there will not be a continuing expansion of pastoral posts, with falling numbers of pupils and reducing numbers of posts of special responsibility, schools must increasingly invest in better patterns of tutorial work.

By this we mean the use of the basic pastoral group of pupils, preferably a mixed ability group formed on their entry to the school, with a teacher to act as their regular form tutor for a period of years. Some schools keep the same tutor with a group throughout their schooling, others prefer to have a change of tutor after the lower and middle school years, arguing that pupils have to learn to cope with changing adult leadership as part of their preparation for work, apart from the fact that it may be better for several members of staff to know a group well. Some members of staff function better with younger or older children also, and can give their best work by being limited to guidance roles in one part of the school.

The following outline job specifications for the form tutor have been suggested from various sources.

(1) (a) General administration and daily registration of the tutor group.
(b)   To know and be directly responsible within the school for each individual pupil within the tutor group.
(c)   To be the 'first line of action' in helping each pupil to cope with his difficulties. Sometimes this will demand disciplinary response, at other times the offering of a listening ear or helping hand, at others the sharing of ideas and experience.
(d)   To communicate essential information to senior colleagues, particularly on attendance and standards of work.
(e)   To be a 'resource person' to other members of staff. The tutor has first-hand knowledge of his pupils which may be valuable to other members of staff.
(f)   To record essential information for the pupils' personal files and ensure that this record is kept up to date.
(g)   To be observant for signs of illness or neglect, injury or over-tiredness, poor eyesight and hearing, changes in friendships, and problems with money.
(h)   To co-ordinate the subject reports and give a coherent report on the pupil.
(i)   To make himself known to the family of each pupil in his group.
(2) (a) To provide the leadership, example, discipline and care ideally exercised by the head of a family group. Each child ought to feel valued.
(b)   To develop a good relationship with each individual child, so that all pupils feel able to bring personal problems to be discussed. Attention has to be given to quiet as well as dominant children.
(c)   To develop loyalty and unity within the group and the house or

year making it an efficient unit within the school. A balance has to be sought between academic and pastoral needs and demands.
(d) To be a link between the child in the group and other staff. The tutor is the foundation of pastoral care, linked with the care of subject teachers and pastoral staff.

The following ways for the form tutor to achieve these aims have been listed in a number of schools.

(1) *Information*. He will seek to have useful and appropriate information about each child. Some familiarity with the child's background is essential—interests, aspirations, problems, successes and crises like bereavement. In this there will necessarily be close liaison with the year head.

(2) *Parents*. He will endeavour to meet parents, particularly those who do not respond to invitations to school functions.

(3) *Supervision of progress*. He will keep a regular watch over the general work and progress of each child, by looking at exercise books, by informal discussion about different subjects and by listening to staff comments about the child. Encouragement and insistence on standards should go together and homework has to be checked.

(4) *Records*. He will keep accurate records of the pupils, not only to achieve administrative efficiency, but also because the need to write constructively about the child promotes positive thought about him. It is important that information on each child is well recorded; staff changes necessitate this and when references and leaving reports are required we need a picture of the pupil's whole school history.

(5) *Appearance*. He will watch for the general tidiness and cleanliness of each child. Deterioration in general behaviour is often accompanied by slackness in dress and appearance. Welfare services may be required for children in need.

(6) *Care of tutorial room*. He will encourage the group to think of the tutorial room as the home of the group which should be tidy and attractive. He will encourage sensible standards of conduct within the room even when he is not present.

(7) *Leadership*. Various responsibilities will be shared by pupils.

(8) *Administrative efficiency*. Routine duties may include: registration; latecomers; dinners; reports; letters to and from parents; medicals.

As in every profession there are varying qualities of teachers, and it is inevitable that there will be a small proportion of lazy and inefficient members of staff. There will also be some good academic teachers who will find it too demanding or difficult to be good form tutors. Some schools have successfully made the selection of form tutors a matter of prestige and there can be competition to be appointed to this extra duty. Other schools appoint tutors in pairs to a larger group of pupils; and others again limit tutorial work to experienced staff only, even when it means larger form groups of twenty-five or more.

Certain things are essential. There must be proper support, usually through pastoral heads, who should seldom have a form themselves, and who will be available for sharing tutorial work and for co-operating with tutors on pupils' individual problems. There must also be in-service training. Since colleges and universities seldom seem to train teachers adequately in their basic pastoral roles, schools will need to use local education authority courses or their own school-based courses, as has already been discussed in Chapter 1. Observation is a learned skill, and even sensitivity can be improved through training. Hopefully, there will also be a well-managed timetable, ensuring that form tutors have worthwhile time with their pupils, in addition to whatever class teaching they take with the pupils. Thirty minutes a day is commonly allocated for registration, administrative tasks and discussion and interviewing time.

Many schools have a weekly tutorial period of the same length as a normal lesson and, if a year group is timetabled for a tutorial period at the same time, a useful pattern emerges. The year head, with a group of colleagues and a cohort of children of the same age group, can arrange small group work for some, counselling interviews for individuals or groups, careers lectures and health education teaching in a flexible and developing system. Each staff team ideally, then, has some teachers experienced in health and careers education and some in counselling and group-work skills. We have seen excellent examples of this pattern of tutorial work develop over the years in schools which have the imagination to invite staff to attend courses and develop interests in a co-operative team approach—a true repertoire of counselling and guidance.

A simple list of possible themes for use in form period discussion times can be as follows.

(1) School organisation and the main points of its philosophy.

(2) Roles of headmaster, deputy headmaster, senior master/mistress, heads of departments, year tutors, class tutors, office staff, ancillary staff.

(3) Communities: the school and the local community; community loyalties; and the need for co-operation.

(4) The need for school rules: detailed explanations and reasons.

(5) Explanation of school information procedures: the importance of communication with parents through the children; purpose of Parent Teachers Association; link with communication in the community—how people are informed.

(6) Information about extra-curricular activities: e.g. the Duke of Edinburgh's Training Scheme, clubs and local leisure opportunities.

(7) Election of representatives to house/year/school councils; agenda and positive and negative contributions discussed; value and difficulties of consultation.

(8) Support for school functions: e.g. concerts, plays, teams, fundraising.

(9) Discussion on occasional group activities, such as a visit to theatre or concert; making class wall magazines; tape recorded magazines for exchange with other classes or schools; class scrapbooks.

(10) Themes for prepared class/school assemblies.

(11) Educational choices in school; debate on personal options; debating standards.

(12) The use of libraries.

(13) Opportunities and need for service; support for charities; community service.

(14) Careers information and discussions.

(15) The class interviewing invited people—school staff and outsiders. Questions are prepared beforehand and discussion follows the visit.

(16) Personal appearance, cleanliness, dress, fitness and general health.

(17) Reading and listening to human relationships themes referred to in appropriate poems and stories.

(18) Films in local cinemas and television programmes. Health themes arising—e.g. smoking and alcohol.

(19) Criticism of magazines and newspapers.

(20) News items and newspaper cuttings.

(21) Local problems: vandalism, etc.

(22) Family holiday/leisure/moving plans.

(23) How pupils identify with the class, with the school, with the community. Awareness by each child:
of himself, his strengths and weaknesses;
of himself with the family;
of himself within the form and in relation to his peers;
of himself within his year group;
of himself with the community.

(24) Friendships in the class and school; the need to give as well as take; loneliness, and the needs of others.

(25) Individual interviews with pupils, particularly on standards of work.

We have many examples of schools which have developed a great deal of such material for use in tutorial time. Some have detailed five-year plans with resource banks of questionnaires, activity cards, photographs and other material. The purpose of this work is to enable the pupils and tutor to know and trust each other better, to provide a safety valve for problems and school stresses, to improve motivation for learning, and hopefully to develop the children as individuals.

The following have been suggested as the major elements in programmes of education in personal relationships. Whilst many references to these will arise in form discussions, it is likely that a deeper and more co-ordinated approach will arise in many areas of subject teaching, preferably with form discussions used to follow up and reinforce what has been taught and discussed elsewhere.

(1) Values and morals
(2) Learning and motivation
(3) Family life and parenthood
(4) Adolescence and health
(5) Authority and responsibilities
(6) Society and communities
(7) Sexuality
(8) Friends and acquaintances
(9) Personality and identity
(10) Communication and sociability

This question of a co-ordinated approach to the teaching of such themes is developed further in Appendix H.

The following subjects are among the more difficult discussion themes in our experience, and many head teachers prefer to have planned discussion and teaching in depth on these themes taken by selected staff. The average person's general knowledge on these topics is often insufficient to deal with the testing questions of the adolescents concerned.

(1) Agression and prejudice
(2) Sexually transmitted diseases
(3) Homosexuality
(4) Deviance and abnormalities
(5) Mental illness
(6) Sex education

The following health themes are often left out of teaching schemes.

(1) Alcohol education
(2) Smoking information
(3) Home safety
(4) Child development
(5) Parenthood
(6) Common ailments and illnesses
(7) Obesity and diet
(8) The handicapped
(9) Community health

Reviewing these approaches to discussion work brings us back to counselling and again to the in-service training and preparation of teachers. Tutorial and class discussion should be valued by the pupils. If a worthwhile co-ordinated programme of topics is discussed, problems can be aired in the security of the group and can often be reduced before they become crises. If bullying, for example, is discussed fully in the first year, this normal fear of young pupils can be reduced, and vigilant tutors will note signals of playground alarms. If public examination pressures and fears are fully debated in earlier years in the security of a familiar tutorial group with a trusted adult, later examination nerves and failures may be avoided. If loneliness and aggression and many other topics are discussed companionably and positively, there will be better understanding of personal feelings, and of the feelings of others. However, all this needs more skills in discussion work and more knowledge of simple group dynamics even than many experienced teachers have, so regular preparation in discussion methods is desirable.

There have been further developments in what is termed 'Active Tutorial Work' in a number of schools; this is a carefully structured approach to developmental group work.* There have been some very successful experiments in this field, reducing discipline troubles and developing the confidence and motivation of youngsters, who work in small groups with prepared teachers.

---

* *Active Tutorial Work*, Lancashire LEA, pub. Blackwells 1979.

4

Pastoral care in colleges

Expectations

Teachers of students in further education and sixth-form colleges
are concerned with training and influencing young people to fit into
the adult society; they should also be concerned with the personal
growth and development of these young people. There will be dispute
as to whether all college teachers accept both these roles as part of their
educational work, but it is likely that society will increasingly see both
roles as part of the function of any institution dealing with young
adults.

Society, to most people, consists of a network of people, a maze of
interpersonal relationships; it consists of the people we know and
meet; it has meaning for most people only when it is related to known
faces and personalities. Colleges should help students to understand
the interpersonal relationships which will make up their society and
thus help them to a mature view of themselves. We are concerned in
helping students to find their personal role and this role comes from
the beliefs and obligations and values which permeate the relationships we make. So, education in personal relationships with older
adolescents is concerned with this personal view of society. However,
students also need to understand how the other kind of society, the
remote society of which government is part, now controls so much of
our lives and so many of our relationships. The State is concerned
with relationships—now in laws—about children, marriage, divorce
and homosexuality; about family planning, and family life in general.
In the kind of society we are creating, which is increasingly influenced
by large corporations and by a remote State, it is essential that we
build up a responsible self-regard amongst students to enable them to
feel whole people in this remote society which they may eventually
help to control.

College staffs should be responsible not only for counselling those
who have personal difficulties, but also for helping students to
comprehend their lives within the community and the state. To

disregard these matters as being beyond the vocational responsibility of a college authority is to abdicate from a caring and teaching role which should exist between older and younger members of any educational community. We are aware, for example, of the influence one particular college has in providing good counselling and tutorial care for immigrant community students, linked with useful adult education for their parents. The same college has a system of developing individual students in basic learning skills, by a withdrawal system to a 'personal development unit'. All this is additional to the normal range of course teaching and tutorial groups with two teacher-counsellors doing half their time on individual counselling as well. There is then a reduction of 'drop-out' rates, and a development of modest talents for the good of the community.

Another college suggests the following analysis as the basis for their work.

What do students say they want from us?

(1) Good teaching: expertise, direction and encouragement.
(2) Friendliness: a concern for individuals.
(3) Reasonable discipline and order, without fuss.
(4) Availability of skilled help when needed: with college, personal and career problems.

Participation

Now that students are legally adult from the age of eighteen *in loco parentis* no longer applies to the older members of a college community. College staff who deal with older students can no longer be regarded as acting as parents, and this has altered the relationship between these older students and college authorities. There may be from this a better mutual understanding of the caring role which college staffs will still be expected to have. To abandon all ideas of offering at least responsible and experienced advice to these young adults would be wrong. Student unions accept that staff can contribute student counselling and guidance, but this contribution is now based more on a basis of equality than on paternal authority.

Students can be resentful of an apparently impersonal institution and yet may glimpse the value of a college as a place for learning to live. They are perhaps resentful of the discipline of school life and may seek responsibility and participation greater than their capabilities. A college will need to accept and mould this youthful and often clumsy demand for freedom and participation. A college which is seen as a place to live and develop and not as a place only for instruction gives ample opportunity for such participation. The way that refectories and social areas are managed, the arrangements for lodging and accommodation, the opportunities for meeting with staff on social occasions and the leisure and sports programme; all these provide the area where participation can become real, and not trivial. It is likely that students will demand much more responsibility in the way that both the social life and the social education in college develop. If we accept that good relationships arise from the way an institution is organised, then young people will be aware of this and will expect to take part in the planning.

The following student problem areas seem to emerge from a number of studies. They are not in order of importance.

(1) Fear of criticism and rejection.
(2) Worry over exams.
(3) Difficulty in concentrating in studying.
(4) Self-consciousness and nervousness in social life.
(5) Study skills lacking:
    (a) note-taking;
    (b) library use;
    (c) allocating time properly;
    (d) coping with different teaching styles;
    (e) reading quickly;
    (f) knowing how to question;
    (g) essay techniques.
(6) Frustration in not having a boy/girl-friend.
(7) Jealousy and anger over relationships.
(8) Worry over alcohol misuse, eating binges, and 'staying in bed to avoid decisions and work'.
(9) General depression and confusion.
(10) Coping with many different teachers.
(11) Making decisions.
(12) Embarrassment in 'speaking badly'.
(13) Health problems.

A college of further education, with many 'O' and 'A' level students, tells its staff that guidance work is essential at the four stages of a student's career:

(1) enrolment—course and career guidance, school liaison and parental advice;
(2) induction—settling in, fees, staff, timetables, social life;
(3) learning—study and other problems, attendance, homework, assessments, accommodation;
(4) leaving—finding employers, preparation for work, adult relationships and family life.

The same college is much concerned with involving its older students in the care and guidance of new students. They also comment on the increasing problems of dealing with accommodation and with overseas students.

Student development committees

A number of colleges have committees of staff and students to consider relationships within the college. Student health and welfare matters, counselling schemes, tutorial arrangements and vocational guidance can be discussed and schemes planned for submission to an academic board or the principal. Such a committee provides a useful practice in democratic procedures, enables worries and grumbles to be reviewed, and provides a joint student-staff approval to college pastoral work. The membership will include representation of all departments, both junior staff and students as well as a few senior staff, student health and accommodation staff, teacher-counsellors and perhaps one or two social agency representatives from the area.

One college suggests, from such a committee that the main problems which stop students functioning well are:
(1) no sense of purpose;
(2) boredom;
(3) lack of self-confidence in studies;
(4) insecurity in personal relationships;
(5) personal and family problems.

Another college group listed student study problems as:
(1) inability to cope with different teaching styles between school and college;
(2) inability to take notes during lessons;
(3) inability to make notes from books;
(4) difficulty in using reference books in essay work;
(5) apprehension about asking questions in class and appearing stupid, often because teachers are assuming previous knowledge;
(6) inadequate essay techniques;
(7) difficulty in organising study and homework time.

The work of tutors

There are many types of tutorial work in colleges; *course tutors* may be responsible for a class or a group of classes in their subject area; *subject tutors* may have a similar function; *personal tutors* may have general pastoral oversight (accommodation, welfare, health and personal problems) over a group of students. Sometimes the two roles are combined and a tutor has oversight of the academic work and a (sometimes nominal) care for students' personal problems; students may doubt whether their problems can be taken to a tutor who is also responsible for their subject marks and for their vocational opportunities through reports and references. Ideally, good teachers can accept and carry out both roles with honesty: in practice, it seems difficult in college settings, more difficult than with pupils in secondary schools.

The attitude of college staff may have something to do with this problem; there is still a strong instructional element in further education teaching and an absence of the pastoral tradition which is commonly accepted in schools. Whilst the college attitude is changing, it has to be agreed that staff and students in colleges do have difficulty in accepting the dual course and personal tutoring roles. For this reason, it is better in many colleges to appoint some of the staff as course tutors, with a clearly defined advisory role, and others as personal tutors. Preferably there will be a team approach with a group of staff allocated to a student group, some as personal tutors, others with academic or administrative roles. This team concept is attractive; it does not leave so strong a demarcation between different tutoring jobs and it brings in all staff for either the course, pastoral or administrative tasks. Under the guidance of a team chairman (not necessarily the head of department) the work can be shared out. Some colleges may timetable this work in such a way that staff with interest in personal tutorial work are shared among many teams, crossing departmental boundaries.

Ideally a majority of the staff will have a personal tutor group and will perhaps also act as course tutors to a second group in their subject department: perhaps, as pastoral understanding grows, the combined course and personal roles can be acceptable to staff and students. If the personal tutoring is limited to occasional 'progress discussions' and to personal counselling of individuals, then it is not essential to know one's personal tutor group in teaching situations, though it is normally an advantage. If a regular programme of education in personal relationships is developed through tutor groups, with a planned development of topics, then it is far better for the tutor also to be subject teacher of his students, for he will be more effective if he knows his students in class-work and in tutorial discussion.

We see that tutor groups can be shaped in many ways and the pattern may change as a college develops as a guidance community as well as an efficient instructional centre. Efficient instruction and academic work depend, in any case, on the guidance community concept being improved.

A good starting point is the establishment of an efficient course tutoring system. If this is developed well, and if in-service training in pastoral work is accepted, then the course tutor system can evolve into a personal tutoring pattern as well, either organised across departmental boundaries (through the team approach) or within departments, if the range of staff interests and concern is wide enough. In all these developments the goodwill and understanding of heads of departments is essential, for they must see that these pastoral developments will improve staff-student relationships and reduce the learning problems of young people.

Within each department there will then be a staff team to act as tutors, perhaps all with a group for personal and course tutoring, perhaps sharing interests and abilities in a team approach. Time for tutorial periods will be required and such time must be purposefully used with departments sharing the development of systematic discussion work. Many colleges allocate one hour a week for this work. One college suggests the following ground rules for tutors:

(1) be impartial and not omnipotent;
(2) avoid gossiping about others with a student and avoid one's own opinions being forced on him;
(3) do not give facile reassurances and neat delineations;
(4) avoid being anxious and do not trivialise;
(5) refer if in doubt and be concise and clear in referring information.

Another college defines the tutor's role as follows:

(1) helping in the personal development of the students;
(2) general oversight of a student's welfare and health;
(3) monitoring academic progress;
(4) liaising with other staff about progress of students;
(5) keeping full records and being a point of reference for jobs, etc;
(6) being the essential link between college administration and the student;
(7) fulfilling a disciplinary role when necessary.

Education in personal relationships

Education in personal relationships is concerned with the interpersonal relationships that one experiences. It is linked with self-regard, for a student builds up a picture of what the actions of others towards him, and his actions towards them, have left him able to believe about himself. The time a student spends in college is immensely important in this matter of self-regard, for he is at his most impressionable age and is learning about emotions and relationships, perhaps without much support. There can be an absence of support because staff may see their students as adults, sometimes not realising that these young adults need as much help as younger pupils in the interpretation of what is happening in their personal lives. Young people in colleges must have counselling support, therefore, but must also be involved in reflection on how college relationships function, as well as considering what society is about.

This means there should be a structure for the presentation of relationships work, and syllabuses, such as the one in Appendix G, may provide a basis for the approach. It is a pity, however, if the only place where such discussion is approved is during General Studies teaching time. Instruction should not be the sole aim of other departments, for relationships are learned as much in talking around an engineering bench, for example, as in a class discussion. There is sometimes a cynicism amongst young people because they see a college solely as a place of instruction. Education in personal relationships in a college is about the kind of society we want students to create after our time. Colleges should surely be as much concerned with attitudes, commitments, and values as they are with vocational skills. So staff that contribute through teaching and discussions must be aware of their own attitudes and values for these may be a basis for their students' understanding of values. Students have a need to identify with someone as they have done in their family setting. Who in the college will be the best person for them to accept as an adviser or confidant? Members of staff who accept such responsibilities and are clear about their own views and beliefs, and who have the ability and opportunity to talk with young people on relationship themes, can be useful and influential. Much of this counselling and discussion work will, in practice, be developed by General Studies departments, but there should be clear encouragement for other departments to share in the work, either through the planned syllabus of work or through the efforts of individual interested lecturers in group or tutorial work or in personal counselling work.

Some colleges have a specialised adviser and lecturer on their staff, known as Student Adviser or Counsellor, and such a person can be useful, but, again, great care must be taken that such specialists do not have all student problems and discussion work presented as being solely their concern. If a specialist assists in staff training, supports other members of staff with tutorial and discussion themes and can encourage and support counselling by other staff, then they can be invaluable; but a full-time counsellor can take away a feeling of responsibility from other staff and can reduce the value of the college as a guidance community, if he or she is the wrong person, e.g. too prone to claim counselling solely as an expert role. If his work is badly planned by the college authority, as well, staff may be discouraged from taking a guidance and counselling role because of thoughtless explanation of the role of a full-time counsellor. Such a counsellor may do well as a co-ordinator, consultant and equal colleague, but never as a secluded expert in charge of the trouble department.

Whether a college can especially select staff to teach or lead discussion on the more emotional aspects of human relationships with students is debatable. Schools need to have such selection, but in colleges most lecturers surely must have an ability to teach informally, so it is likely that most lecturers, especially those concerned with liberal education, will be able to contribute to difficult themes in education in personal relationships. Alternatively, some principals may feel that whilst the great majority of studies in human relationships can be taken by any responsible member of staff, the more controversial and emotional aspects of human relationships are best dealt with by selected staff. In this case, if a college does not have a member of staff particularly suitable for this kind of work, it is often possible to bring in outside counsellors, and group workers, who on a regular visiting basis can be of value in supporting the college staff. The message of such discussions is simple: a satisfying kind of life means having satisfying kinds of relationships and these come from understanding other people. The whole purpose of leadership in such education for living is to facilitate the work of young people in clarifying their understanding of other people. It is in this way that self-confidence grows, and with self-confidence comes ability in relationships, and from this may stem satisfying family and work relationships.

Colleges have developed many ways of extending these discussions with students, either in tutor groups, class teaching or in voluntary discussion groups. One successful method is to invite visitors who have a particular experience or ability. Rather than giving a talk and then being questioned, such visitors are introduced to a small group and left to be provoked and tested by questions. Clearly the number of visitors with the skills to stand this kind of approach must be limited, but their value can be immense. One thinks for example, of the capable young clergyman who may relish this kind of open-ended and difficult approach to his pastoral work. Sometimes authority figures, such as policemen, can be interviewed, and can not only help youngsters to see people away from their stereo-typed roles, but also refresh their own thinking by their nearness to young people who may be speaking with new and considerable frankness.

It is sometimes useful to have regular Brains Trusts. Two or three people can come and make themselves available to a group of students who will have been invited beforehand to prepare questions. The anonymity of a question can give a skilled Brains Trust group an opportunity to put over attitudes which may be helpful. Sometimes discussion-group leaders can act in pairs, and a husband and wife team can be very useful in this way. Then young people glimpse the kind of relaxed interchange that can take place between a happily married young couple talking about love or marriage for example, and can see a relationship in practice; they learn without discussion. Whilst the formal aspects of a discussion may be very limited, the practical value may be considerable.

Some colleges of our acquaintance have developed extensive resources for such discussion work, for tutors to select apropriate news cuttings, questionnaires and other material as aids to talking. Many colleges also have conducted half-day or day conferences for all staff on their tutoring role. Many colleges, also, are now beginning to concern themselves gradually with co-ordinating a health education programme of talks, films and discussions in their tutorials or class teaching.

Careers education

Careers guidance at colleges may at times be weak, for there is an assumption that such guidance has taken place at an earlier stage. Colleges sometimes presume that the choices made on entry are final and unalterable, but this seems to be wrong when so many choices of careers are available. Colleges should offer a continuing guidance system to allow for those who wish to change their courses, an increasing likelihood in future college work, and such guidance can be done by members of staff, as well as by experts from outside. It may be that in a college a student gets the adult help and interpretation which he has perhaps lacked in his home setting and which can direct him towards a better choice of course and career. An occupational identity seems to be increasingly essential in life and it is the basis of so much of our self regard. Whilst one's confidence in relationships is the greatest strength in our ability to deal with life, the kind of occupational identity that we develop gives us our sense of pride and achievement.

Much of the personal counselling work which can develop in a college may well be based in the first place on educational and vocational guidance. Whether personal guidance follows other guidance work depends on the personalities of the staff involved. Students are, of course, completely free to use them or to reject them as reference points for their personal problems.

Counselling schemes

Student counselling schemes can take several forms. A particular group of interested staff may arrange, after preparation and training, to provide a counselling centre where students will know that a rota of counselling staff is available, perhaps at a lunch-time. There is an opportunity then for students with particular problems to choose the tutor they wish to meet in such a scheme. It may be that greater use can also be made of young counsellors selected from the students themselves, working with staff, for there is a growing awareness that many young people have the maturity and ability to counsel their fellows, given proper support. Many colleges are developing such voluntary counselling schemes, organised by staff and student leaders, often with the further safety-valve of a visiting part-time outside counsellor available at times during the week.

Students may comment little, but are likely to value the effort that an institution makes to offer a variety of counselling facilities, and the appreciation is likely to be greater if such schemes are offered in an unostentatious and yet efficient way. It is for students to choose to use such schemes and the disappointments and occasional lack of apparent appreciation have to be accepted. Colleges need safety valves and such schemes supply this need.

College counselling should be seen as preventive in the main, supportive at all times, but hardly curative. It is concerned with preventing or reducing problems, not only with offering counselling at times of crisis. It is essential to see good personal counselling as part of normal development—there are 'normal' problems in most lives. The truly emotionally-sick student needs more expert help and 'abnormal' or clinical counselling should, of course, be referred to experts, though care and support may continue if such expertise is difficult to find. One sees certain stages in a college counselling plan, as follows.

(1) All students have an opportunity to discuss relationships and normal problems in discussion groups, perhaps in general tutorial groups taken by a majority of staff working in teams, or individually, or perhaps in short courses for all students taken by selected staff. A mixture of both types of discussion work may be the best approach.

(2) Personal counselling can follow from this with students seeking any of the tutorial staff they know and trust, but also using a voluntary staff counselling team which is available at regular times.

(3) A small group of two or three staff has deeper counselling training and has time allocated for counselling and discussion work, or a visiting part-time counsellor can act as a further referral point.

A full-time counsellor trained in one of the counselling diploma courses can, of course, fit into such a pattern very well as can accommodation officers and medical officers. A Lancashire Working Party on Student Counselling has produced a rationale for counselling based on the above approach and this is shown in Appendix C.

The fact that a college offers teaching and discussion on human relationships and has personal counselling help available for students needs to be known by students—an obvious point which is sometimes forgotten. Such schemes are sometimes advertised above the students' level; 'Window-dressing' schemes exist which may be valued by the L.E.A., by governors and public, but are not part of the students' world. Good publicity is important, preferably organised by students. Parents also need to have a clear understanding of these schemes. Publicity should aim at presenting a simple caring scheme, avoiding counselling jargon and hints of great expertise.

5

Health and social education

During the 1960s and 1970s, we have seen the gradual emergence of organised teaching concerning health and social themes. These themes have appeared under numerous names within the curriculum, sometimes being taught within timetabled lessons, sometimes spread out through traditional subject departments and tutorial time. The names used for both approaches have constantly changed from Humanities, Civics and Family Life Education in the 1960s, to Moral Education, Social Education, Education for Personal Relationships and Health Education in the 1970s. Many of the areas covered within these broad themes are similar and have increasingly become accepted in most schools as an important part of the curriculum for all children.

There was a tendency in the past for these themes to be dealt with more often with less able or socially inadequate children. This tendency is fast waning as health education (the term more commonly used today) is seen to be to do with promoting positive health for all pupils, rather than concerned just with problems. Schools have become more and more aware of the need to reassess their role in society and the way they prepare children for the future, for health and social education is not an alternative to, or even a contender with, traditional academic education. It is a natural component of any education that prepares children for adulthood and for working and social life.

Increasingly over the last few years the Government has urged that this area of the curriculum be given attention and seen as an important component of normal schooling.

Government reports*

(References are numbered and listed on pp. 58 and 59.)
(1) In 1976–77 the Expenditure Committee reported in three volumes of report and evidence on preventive medicine.[1] This has been

---

* This section is reprinted from *Monitor* by permission.

answered in a White Paper from the Government on 'Prevention and Health', presented in Parliament in December, 1977.[2]

The report

The recommendations were:

'Health education should begin as early in the life of the individual as possible. However, the teaching at home must be supplemented by more and better teaching at school, supported by more effective community service.'

(Report—para. 80 and recommendation 4 para. 309)

'Pupils at both primary and secondary school should undertake a period of physical exercise, whether a team game or not, at least once a week. Wherever this is not the norm we strongly commend it to the authorities responsible for curricula.'

(Report—para. 260 and rec. 50 para. 309)

'Children should be treated as first priority for preventive programmes.' (Report—para. 301 and rec. 58 para. 309)

'Health Education should be taught (to teachers) in refresher courses.' (Report—para. 83 and rec. 6 para. 309)

All of these recommendations were supported by the Government in the White Paper.[2]

The following recommendations were put forward by the Select Committee and are still under discussion or partly approved of by the Government:

'We are, however, concerned that a large number of teachers attend family planning and other courses at their own expense because their Education Authorities are not prepared to sponsor them. We recommend that teachers should be sponsored for such courses.'

(Report—para. 82 and rec. 5 para. 309)

'Health Education should form a more important part of the basic training of teachers.' (Report—para. 83 and rec. 6 para. 309)

'There should be more sex education in schools, with particular emphasis on the importance of responsible and loving relationships, provided that the views of the parents have been considered in this context.' (Report—para. 174 and rec. 33 para. 309)

'That more resources should be devoted to an intensive campaign for dental health education, particularly in schools.'

(Report—para. 228 and rec. 37 para. 309)

'The relevant Government Departments (i.e. the DHSS and the DES) should actively promote the practice of physical exercise.'
(Report—para. 260 and rec. 47 para. 309)

(2) *The White Paper*[2]

The White Paper mentions that the document 'Education in Schools' (The Green Paper Cmnd. 6869) and the first report of the Select Committee on Violence in the Family both stress the need for education in parenthood for both boys and girls. It stresses that the gains from a preventive approach to health include gains for the individual, for the health services, for the health professions and for the economy. (See para. 258 of the White Paper.)

It also says:

'Education and guidance on healthy living are necessary both at home and at school to counteract some of the undesirable pressures to which the younger generation is subjected.'   (White Paper—para. 46)

'Teachers of many subjects can contribute to sex education. They can often plan together a balanced programme appropriate to the needs of each age group. In-service courses, in which teachers can discuss changing health and social needs and perhaps come to terms with their own feelings about them, are valuable. The Departments (DHSS and DES) therefore hope that as resources permit, Local Education Authorities will seriously consider allowing teachers to attend in-service health education courses.'   (White Paper—para. 179)

(3) *Violence to children*

The report from the Select Committee on Violence, entitled 'Violence to Children'[3] States:

'We believe, as our predecessors did (the Select Committee on Violence in Marriage) that much more should be done in the school curriculum to ensure that all pupils receive some education in the skills of parenthood. By this we do not mean simply abstract instruction in the physiological mechanisms of conception and childbirth, but learning about what young children are really like.'   (Para. 60)

'We recommend that the Government, whether through the DHSS or the DES, should ensure that education for parenthood is available for boys and girsl of *all* levels of intellectual ability.'   (Para. 60).

(4) Violence in marriage

The Select Committee on Violence in Marriage[4] recommended that

much more attention be given within our schools and further education system to the problems of domestic conflict. (Para. 16).

(5) *DES circulars*

The DES circulated all LEAs and training establishments with a
memoranda on health education.[5] It:

(a) brings to the reader's attention the new handbook 'Health
Education in Schools'; (Para. 1)

(b) quotes 'Education in Schools' (the Green Paper) as saying:

'Education for good, healthy and happy personal relationships
begins in the home, but through childhood and adolescence
young people will be greatly influenced by teaching and example
at school.' (Para. 2)

(c) lists reports available mentioning Health Education; (Para. 3–5)

(d) states that these have implications to teachers and the trainers of
teachers; (Para. 6)

(e) mentions the following curriculum development projects:

—'Living Well' 12–18 years, by the Health Education Council;
—'All About Me' and 'Think Well' 5–13 years, by the Schools
Council;
—Schools Council Health Education Project 13–18;
—'Health Education', Working Paper 57 from the Schools
Council; (Para. 7)

(f) mentions the need for collaboration between education and the
health services; (Para. 8)

(g) accepts that individual L.E.A.s will respond in their own way.
(Para. 9)

(6) In the DES circular on the curriculum[6] it is important to note that
this area of the curriculum is specifically asked about in Section
B as follows.

Section B. Curriculum balance and breadth
B5 How does the authority help secondary schools provide for (1)
moral education, (2) health education, (3) careers education, (4) social
education through community links etc. *whilst giving adequate attention
to the basic educational skills?* What part is played by the idea of a core or
protected part of the curriculum?
B6 How do schools promote racial understanding?'

(7) Nutrition Education

In the report on nutrition education[7] the following is stated:

'We identified teachers as one of the key groups with influence in imparting nutrition education. The role of teachers is only one part of the total contribution to nutrition education made by schools and other educational establishments.'   (Para. 3.6.1)

'It is also important that a good example be set by schools in all other aspects of school life (for example in school tuckshops or vending machines)'.   (Para. 3.6.6.)

'In order to provide the best nutrition education in schools, it is clearly desirable that teachers, particularly of Home Economics and the biological sciences, should be properly equipped.'   (Para. 5.5.2)

(8) Drug misuse

In the DES report on drug misuse among children of school age[8] it states:

'Those responsible for the school curriculum should consider the inclusion of education about the right use of drugs and the danger of experimentation and misuse in the context of general health and social education.   (Recommendation 1)

(a) LEAs should encourage schools . . . to review and define their policies and attitudes on such matters as:

The development of a system of pastoral care designed to ensure a continuing awareness and concern for the welfare of the individual.

(b) LEAs should consider the desirability where necessary of initiating co-operation with other local statutory services, the police and voluntary bodies concerned with the welfare of young people, and of ensuring that the support services available to the community at large are linked with the support services within the school.'

(9) The Court Report

The Court Report[9] states:

'We warmly welcome the tendency, especially in secondary schools, for the nexus of topics connected with health education to be taken as a serious subject of study and discussion by senior teachers whose experience of life is as important to their success as their mastery of fact. We have been impressed by the quality of the teaching materials created by the Schools Council project on Health Education for children aged 5–13'.

'We urge that society should not leave the job solely to the schools.'
(Para 10.31 Vol. 1 P153)

'Attention to improving an individual's general ability to cope with life is the chief issue and should in any case be a primary objective of schools.'

'. . . Emphasis should be placed on skills in interpersonal relationships, in communication and in helping children to understand themselves and the world around them.' (Para. 10.35 Vol. 1 P155).

(10) *Alcoholism*

The report of the Advisory Committee on Alcoholism[10] states:

'1. Health education designed to alert people to the dangers of alcohol and to discourage excessive drinking should be encouraged and expanded.' (Rec. 1)

'2. At school a child will be increasingly influenced by his peers as well as by his teachers. Here the form and content of education about drinking can be structured with a view to countering, where appropriate, accepted attitudes.' (Page 6)

(11) *Health Education in Schools*

'Health Education in Schools'[11] discusses health; the health services; Biology and health education; communicable diseases; pollution; toxic materials; accidents; dental health; drugs; alcohol; smoking; sex education; mental health and health education in schools.

(12) From these publications some general points emerge which perhaps could be stated as follows:

(a) At a time when prevention of ill health rather than treatment of ill health is seen as very important, schools are regarded as very important areas for health education.

(b) Health education is very different today from what it was ten or twenty years ago, and now incorporates material relevant to good social relationships, identity and parental roles.

(c) Schools should not feel they have little influence. They may be regarded as only one agency among many doing the same health education work, but they are seen as crucially important in this work if other agencies are to succeed.

(d) On a number of occasions quality rather than quantity in health education is mentioned. Basic skills are a part of health education and do not conflict with the teaching of it. (It has been suggested that health education facilitates good learning by attempting to rectify factors which affect learning.)

(e) The corporate influence of all agencies is expected to have effects.

(f) There is a great need for the prevention of ill health, and children are a crucial group to educate.

(g) If education is to have breadth and relevance, health and social education should not be used to replace academic areas. The curriculum should be balanced in such a way as to incorporate health/social education for children of both sexes and all ability ranges.

(h) In-service training is essential in this area of the curriculum.

(13) Appendix H is a working paper by the Health Education Committee of HM Inspectorate (December 1978).

The aims

Whatever name is ascribed to this work within the curriculum, the following broad aims of health and social education are often suggested.

To help pupils to find information about human behaviour, to examine the values which people have found lead to personal happiness and stability in our society, and to encourage pupils to develop standards in personal morality. Specific points include the following.

(1) To encourage positive attitudes in pupils towards their own personal health and the acquiring of healthy habits.

(2) To give pupils some knowledge of the causes of disease, the effects of self neglect and the hazards of the environment, and to inform them of appropriate preventative measures.

(3) To help pupils to come to terms with their own physical and emotional development.

(4) To help pupils to develop stable relationships with others, to accept other people and to appreciate the value of tolerance.

(5) To awaken awareness in pupils of their responsibilities towards others in relation to the world they live in.

(6) To prepare pupils for the responsibilities of marriage and family life

(7) To offer pupils opportunities to make reasoned choices in matters that could affect their well-being.

The scope

This area of the curriculum is concerned with helping young people to develop mentally, emotionally, morally and socially in order to be able to benefit fully from their lives at school and after school, and to be able to relate to others adequately. Traditionally, this area of education has been seperated into 'boxes' and called one of the names discussed earlier (see p. 46). It may appear as 'health education', in which case many teachers may not feel this is their responsibility. It may appear as 'family life education', in which case it can often be left in a school to the home economics staff. We do not believe that the name matters. We do believe however that this aspect of education is central to the role of the school and facilitates all of the traditional aims of schools in the basic skills and academic areas of the curriculum. We equally believe that it is a central part of the role of every teacher and cannot be left to certain departments in schools, or certain teachers.

The implicit curriculum

Health education is concerned with producing good health in the widest possible terms. Implicit in this is the fact that health is not attainable by people knowing a large number of facts; it is bound up in the lifestyle of individuals, in the relationships which they have, and in the image that they have of themselves.

The school has a major effect on children in all these contributory aspects to health. From the earliest age the child learns whether he is valued by others, for the child at school is taught as much by the relationships and social order of the school as by specific lessons. This picture of himself develops in early childhood and grows during schooling. Undoubtedly the self-image is moulded considerably by the school and has an effect on the later health and social ability of young people.

The school also develops or divides relationships between children at all ages. The natural process of schooling children places children in groups. The way that the teacher handles these groups, and helps the individual to develop competency in relationships, must affect the later life of the young person.

Children in school reflect today a wide variety of lifestyles and value systems of the type of society that now exists. The school, by its structures, can ignore this diversity of opinion and lifestyle or can openly offer the opportunity, through pastoral systems, for children to discuss their development into autonomous human beings. The school has a vital role in producing children and young people who will eventually be as capable as possible to make their own decisions, but at the same time to make them with due consideration of the effect upon others. The good school will do all in its power to assist children towards this balance of autonomy and responsibility.

The explicit curriculum and the co-ordinator

The majority of schools recognise that some work is carried out within the curriculum concerning health education and attempt to make sure that it follows a logical and sensible pattern. One immediate problem is the wide diversity of themes that may need to be covered (*see* Appendix G). Although it is clearly difficult to include such work as a separate series in an already full syllabus, many of the themes are essential in preparation for work and family life and are very relevant to the lives of pupils. Much of the work will already be included in departmental subject areas, but co-ordination and reinforcement are obviously essential; head teachers may consider appointing a senior member of staff to co-ordinate the teaching of this work, and to guide other staff as to the best way of developing this teaching and discussion work. Certain aspects of the syllabus may be reinforced by help from colleagues in other services, especially in the Health Service.

The co-ordinator could gradually be responsible for developing the quality of the health, social and moral education of young people in the school. Among his responsibilities could be the following.

(1) Monitoring who is teaching what throughout the school and initially analysing the results obtained. He will look specifically for those classes receiving repetition of certain topics, for classes who receive no health education at all with certain topics and for those topics which are not covered at all in the curriculum.

(2) Drawing heads of departments together for consultation on the appropriate allocation of certain topics.

(3) Looking into the feasibility of a core course in health and social education for certain age groups, and discussing the possibility of initiating such a course.

(4) Looking for new scope for initiative within the wide range of health/social/moral education.

(5) Acting as a staff tutor: to collect new material on resources, training courses, etc., and to arrange for previews of materials.

(6) Sounding out the feasibility of in-service training for staff in up-to-date methods of health and social education, and setting up such courses.

(7) Linking the health education and the pastoral work in the school.

(8) Initiating work with parents which will involve them in the school's health/social/moral education work.

(9) Arranging meetings with other professionals in the area, in liaison with the pastoral care staff, in order to plan lunch-time or other short meetings, where the co-ordination in key health areas could be discussed.

(10) Finding suitable speakers or tutors in the area who could be used in school.

(11) Setting up arrangements to record radio and TV programmes, and to make these available to staff.

(12) Liaising with other schools in the area to compare work and discuss the feasibility of joint in-service training.

Responsibility for health/social/moral education covers so diffuse an area that it cannot be shared among several people without co-ordination. Experience shows without co-ordination there is often confusion, due to poorly delineated objectives. If a co-ordinator is appointed within a school, he or she may need to be of sufficient status in the school (e.g. head of department or senior teacher) to be able to co-ordinate efficiently. The post may be given as an extra responsibility to a senior teacher or department head who is interested in this field, or the appointment may be the responsibility of a scaled post, or of a deputy head.

A co-ordinator will need some of the following skills.

(1) *Tact* is perhaps the most essential skill, as without this quality it is unlikely that he will be able to encourage people to modify the work they are doing.

(2) *Organising ability*—an ability to synthesise at every level.

(3) *An understanding of basic health education.* It is possible for the co-ordinator to be trained, and it is also necessary that he should be willing to specialise to some extent, and to do further training.

(4) *Creativity.* He needs to initiate new ventures and to refine older methods and to inspire staff to have confidence in new ventures.

(5) *An ability to work well with young people.* The co-ordinator must be able to give a practical demonstration of the work he is initiating, and not merely administer.

(6) *Sensitivity* to the constraints working against staff, to inability of some staff to teach in certain ways, to offer support to staff where it is needed.

A method of co-ordinating health education

The following method may assist in assessing what is already being done in a school.*

(1) Have photocopies made of the topics listed in section (20) of Appendix G, or of a similar chosen list, and letter or number each item. Distribute to all members of staff, or to all subject departments.

(2) Request staff to indicate when topics are taken in subject teaching, and in which classes. Collate the results as follows.

* From TACADE head teacher's manual on Curriculum Planning by J. C. P. Cowley, by permission of TACADE.

Class	Science	R.E.	History	(etc.)	Tutorial Period
3B	W Z M	E J F	Y 3 E J		E
3C	W T M	Z	Y 3 E J		E L

(3) From the grids you will be able to analyse at least:
(a) which classes are constantly getting some topics;
(b) which classes have very little health education;
(c) some subjects where topics are being covered which seem totally unrelated;
(d) by comparing vertical grids, you can see if it is likely that the same topics are covered year after year.

If you have appointed a co-ordinator, he or she will be able to analyse the grid further and discuss aspects of it with members of staff, attempting to refine the work being carried out and thus both increasing the careful organisation of health education and possibly saving curriculum time.

In-service education with teachers

There has been very little initial training of teachers in this aspect of the curriculum. A large number of very helpful and beneficial in-service schemes have been developed over the last decade which have provided the opportunity for teachers to discuss this aspect of the curriculum and the methods and organisation related to it.

Some local education authorities have developed extensive schemes of in-service education. Lancashire for example, has training throughout the year in different aspects and at different levels of this area of the curriculum.

Many national organisations have attempted to support teachers in this area of the curriculum by providing in-service education courses. The Marriage Guidance Council has for many years, run courses on education in personal relationships for teachers. The Schools Council has initiated two health education projects, both which have been supported by the Health Education Council. This organisation has particularly supported and financed the development of in-service education manuals. These are comprehensive in-service education packs for the use of individual school staffs as school-based training.

A strategy of in-service courses was developed by TACADE which aimed at attempting to help teachers to look at the organisation of health, social and personal education in the curriculum and which has been developed through many local education authorities. This form of in-service consisted of three parts outlined below.

(1) *Head Teachers' Seminar*

The main purpose of this seminar was to give head teachers time to think through the implications of health education curriculum planning and co-ordination. In the planning of a structured approach it was vital that the concept of having experts telling people what to do was challenged, as head teachers obviously have a wealth of experience upon which to draw. A carefully structured day was developed during which the experience of head teachers could be used, certain issues focused upon and then these same issues related back to their experience. A tutor was provided who could draw out the implications of the comments and work of the head teachers.

(2) *Co-ordinators' course*

Following the head teachers' seminar, the co-ordinators' course was provided for health education co-ordinators from the same schools as the head teachers. The course aimed to look in detail at the practical role of co-ordinators, various methods which could be used in the teaching of health education, the use of visitors in schools and methods of preparing schemes of work with realistic objectives. Much of this work was carried out through experimental learning.

(3) *Professional development workshops*

The workshops aimed to provide follow-up training for the co-ordinators who had already been on the co-ordinators' course. They have proved one of the major innovations to come out of this structured approach to in-service training. Their underlying theoretical concepts are as follows.

(a) In order to fit new considerations into present work practice, any learning experience should use the teacher's own experience. The workshop should be planned in such a way as to give sufficient time to focus on important considerations, concepts and practices. In this way the idea of a teacher-training 'expert', who tells teachers what they should know about health education and what they should do, is avoided.

(b) Much theory from both the medical and, more importantly, the behavioural sciences is pertinent and should be applied to health education. At the same time it must be recognised that much educational theory is not being applied. The workshops, through a series of structured tasks, aim to develop theoretical concepts alongside practical application.

The following areas need to be covered during the workshops.

(a) *Pragmatic issues*: for example concerning the use of visitors in schools, such as looking at why visiting speakers are frequently used in health education, clarifying the perceptions of the teachers at the workshop about visitors and working towards more appropriate ways of using visitors.

(b) *Medical issues*: for example, to try to clarify what research on certain topics has shown and the implications of that research, as in the implications for alcohol education of research into drinking patterns.

(c) *Attitudes*: to give teachers the opportunity to assess (rather than just discuss) their own attitudes on particular topics and how these attitudes may interact with their teaching.

(d) *Methods*: opportunities are given for styles of teaching (such as group work or discussion work), teaching related to objectives (such as teaching facts, attitudes or skills), and the acquisition of skills (such as sensitivity skills) to be explored and, in some cases, learned.

Health education is unlike many other subjects. Most of those now teaching it trained in one or more other subjects. There is, therefore, a growing recognition among teachers that if the subject is to be tackled effectively, then the theory, methods and practical implications need to be explored again. At a time when the curriculum in schools is being refined and in-service training critically examined, perhaps a movement towards carefully worked out, structured and trial-tested in-service training is to be welcomed.

References

1 First Report for the Expenditure Committee 1976–77, *Preventive Medicine*, Vols I, II, III, HMSO, 17.2.1977.

2 *Prevention and Health*, DHSS, DES, SO, WO, Presented to Parliament December 1977. HMSO 1977.

3 First Report from the Select Committee on Violence in the Family 1976–77, *Violence to Children*, Report 26.4.1977, HMSO.

4 Report from the Select Committee on Violence in the Family 1974–75, *Violence in Marriage*, HMSO.

5 DES 15/77, Welsh Office 8/77 Joint Administrative Memorandum, *Health Education in Schools*, 7.12.1977 (circulated to LEAs and training establishments).

6 DES 14/77, Welsh Office 185/77, *Local Authority Arrangements for the School Curriculum*, 29.11.1977.

7 *Nutrition Education,* Joint Report of the British Nutrition Foundation, DHSS and the Health Education Council, HMSO, 1977.

8 *Drug Misuse among Children of School Age,* DES, Welsh Office, 1977.

9 *Fit for the Future* (The Court Report), Report of the Committee on Child Health Services, HMSO, Vol I, 1977.

10 *Advisory Committee on Alcoholism: Report on Prevention,* DHSS, 1977.

11 *Health Education In Schools,* DES, published by HMSO, 1977.

See also:

Prevention and Health: Everybody's Business, HMSO, 1976.

Curriculum Paper 14—Health Education, HMSO, Scotland.

The Structure of the Curriculum in the Third and Fourth Year of the Scottish Secondary School, Scottish Education Department, HMSO, 1977.

6

The management of normal problems

Who is at risk?

Attempts have been made to list a number of young people who are likely to be at risk. If this is known, and providing we do not type-cast pupils and appoint them too early to a clinical career, we can be watchful and sensitive with those at risk. They include children from families where the parents have marital difficulties, particularly where there is separation and divorce; those in care; those with severe health problems and those who are physically handicapped; immigrant pupils of all types, particularly where there are racial differences, but not forgetting those who move from one part of the country to another; dull and immature pupils; the sexually precocious; the fearful, withdrawn and aggressive pupils.

Also included among the list of vulnerable young people are those who are at the onset of puberty; those who change school; those who are timid and liable to be led by others; pupils who constantly argue for independence from parents; and those without ambition or ideas for future occupation. We can add young people who fall in love very early and very genuinely—they will obviously be at risk of deep hurt; and we must consider those who face religious problems, perhaps with the demands of their parents contrasting with the confusion of their own independence of thought. We must also consider individuals who find difficulty in coping with freedom and choice; pupils at certain ages are given responsibilities and are expected to make choices in school work, but sometimes they can be at risk without the staff realising there is considerable disturbance.

There must be puzzlement in a school as to whether counselling is intended for students with problems or whether it is something which 'normal' pupils need. It is essential to realise that all people have problems, and there are stages in the development of all the pupils in a school when various problems arise. Coping with problems is, in fact, part of the process of maturing, but it is essential to offer support and guidance to all pupils of a school, not presuming that the more intelligent and well-spoken are somehow immune. Teachers will balance what is needed; most problems of normal pupils can be ventilated and help can be given through group discussion work and through relationships which class tutors and subject teachers can offer incidentally. The amount of help which pupils with greater problems require is another matter; they take a disproportionate amount of time. A troubled pupil may be aggressive or withdrawn, inarticulate or voluble, grudging and unbelieving that the world of school can have any relevance. This is where skills are required and there is a temptation for most of the counselling to veer towards the problem pupil, but a balance must be kept between 'normal' and 'special' problems.

Ordinary problems of normal life

Although we seem in our experience never to have met a tidily listed problem, the following normal or everyday problems may be considered part of adolescence, which itself can be divided into several stages.

Puberty and physical development

Pupils need explanation and reassurance, usually in teaching or discussion settings, about the characteristics of puberty and about the wide variations in individual physical development. There can be surprising ignorance and even alarm over differing rates of growth and about varying sexual development, and a planned programme of health education should be part of every secondary school's curriculum, including sex education and an understanding of adolescence. Group discussions can relieve worries, and individual counselling and explanations can follow if required.

Emotional development

Learning how to cope with emotions is a normal part of growing up, but it can be discomforting. Young people find it more difficult than adults to conceal their developing emotions, and the processes of learning about and coping with such feelings as jealousy and anger may need explanation and support.

Sexuality

Sexuality is a major part of our personality and it can be so varied a factor that explanation and supportive discussion can be helpful to young people. A wide and intelligent understanding of sexuality, and indeed an understanding of sensuality also, can help towards a mature use of sex, and can attempt to balance the cheapening and crude presentation of sex that the mass media often presents to youngsters.

Intelligence

At some stage of our life we have to come to terms with our personal level of intelligence, and with our position in the intellectual pecking order. This usually happens during adolescence, and caring schools will ensure that the truth of one's position in a competitive system is kindly as well as accurately presented. An understanding of one's ability may better come through guidance and tutorial interviews and discussions perhaps than from crude streaming and coldly published marks' lists. The possibility for late development of intellectual ability must be explained, and some measure of intellectual success is every pupil's right.

Independence

It is necessary and right for every adolescent to grow gradually away from dependence on their family, and to become independent. This is a frequent source of friction and misunderstanding, and yet such independence is natural, and can still be linked with family affection if school and home jointly help in the process. This is one of the main areas of need in counselling and discussion work in schools, and can sometimes be the area that leads to misuse of drugs and alcohol, as youngsters protest their independence in ways they know will affront and challenge their families and teachers.

Personal relationships

Good personal relationships are fundamental in enjoyment of life, and are largely determined by family upbringing, for the confidence that comes from a happy family setting may be the main factor in ability to cope easily with relationships.

Relationships with parents are often difficult in adolescence and young people may need to have their parents' viewpoints put to them objectively. Adolescence may often match a testing time in their parents' lives, and counselling or discussion groups can be helpful in keeping problems in perspective and in ensuring the parents' views and needs are comprehended by their children.

Relationships with peer groups can produce varied pressures. The need of young people to conform to their peer group culture can conflict with family teaching and with the youngster's need to try out differing roles and moods. Again support can sometimes be helpful, and if young people have difficulties in relating to contemporaries of either sex guidance can be essential.

Social competence

Our ability to know how to conduct social relationships with competence is part of adolescent education. Perhaps knowing *how* to cope with social situations is more important than we realise, as is the ability to know *how* to talk to people, for if we cannot express our feelings we are unlikely to have listeners.

Learning

The processes of learning are, we feel, still underestimated and induction programmes and study skills lessons are a vital part of pastoral care. We have too high a proportion of school pupils who feel they cannot learn, and who are therefore our opponents in education. The greatest source of problems in school and colleges probably lies in learning problems.

A sixth form once wrote that the stresses they faced in learning included: cramped conditions and poor facilities, pressure of large numbers, the interruptions of poor discipline, difficult relationships with some teachers, heavy demands of homework and examinations and too much responsibility for younger pupils.

Self-consciousness

Shyness and temporary worries and moods need understanding and all pupils need occasional help in keeping their self-consciousness and occasional gaucheries or crudities in perspective. Sometimes this will lead to individual counselling, but more often the best support and teaching comes in group discussions we feel.

Values

The family based roots of individual values do not prevent schools and colleges having an important part to play in resolving pupils' and students' confusion over personal philosophies for life.

Family life

Many details of family life occasion temporary stresses: arguments over pocket money, TV-watching, levels of pop music noise, dealing with the elderly, times of reaching home at night; all are ordinary but can become overstressed and may need support or advice at the time.

Bereavements arise and are normal also but, again, can seem overwhelming at the time, and need help from an adult in keeping them in perspective.

Self-esteem

How difficult it is to write helpfully on this important theme. We all have a view of ourselves, partly created by the responses of others to us, and schools have a vital, and sometimes underestimated, role in helping young people to build a sense of identity. They need to experience success, to learn to manage failure, and to build sufficient confidence in themselves to persevere and to achieve, to trust and to accept trust, and to try out a variety of roles and responses. Teachers are mirrors for young people in this, and can be very influential in the lives of young people.

In all this pattern of ordinary life, some events will need little help from teachers, much will be coped with in family and peer group settings. Our task is not to intervene or interfere in every stage of young peoples' lives; rather should we be ready to support the casualties, the ones who can sometimes be emotionally crippled by events that others take in their stride; and at all times we should be interpreting the difficulties of normal living, preferably before they normally occur. No-one matures without conflict, but we should ensure that the conflict is kept within bounds.

Some problems are lifelong, of course, and are a permanent part of someone's personality. All we can do at times is to help people to live with the inevitable, perhaps offering strategies for coping day to day. Young people may have limited abilities with relationships because of lack of opportunity and experience in making childhood friendships and it may be difficult to repair the gaps. Others may have an unattractive appearance or unattractive behavioural traits that they cannot alter. Others may have a lack of resource and ability to persevere with relationships, making them always escape from any intimacy; or they may be unable to guard their tongue, always having to blurt out a retort. Our help may be limited, and perhaps most assistance can come from their peer group friends or acquaintances rather than from adults.

Difficulties in counselling

There is a danger that some staff of an institution will see their role as being only instructors and purveyors of knowledge, and will look to others to deal with the personal side of their pupils' lives. There is sometimes an implication that counselling and guidance work is something for the difficult or maladjusted child, and that average children are unlikely to need much pastoral support. This is often linked with the feeling that children who are academically bright are unlikely to have many problems.

Effective counselling means careful planning and structuring. This is against the inclination of many who like informal, implicit and relaxed approaches, and who fear hierarchies and systems. Yet without systems too many gaps arise and caring relationships with individuals and groups may be ineffectual because administration is poor. Counselling is most effective in schools which are carefully prepared to offer a range of counselling support, so that there are many opportunities and facilities for every child, including work with groups as well as individuals. Status can be a difficult factor in a good guidance system; if the status of those who do pastoral work is set too high or too low it can cause jealousies or problems which may reduce the value of the work done.

Senior staff may refuse to delegate responsibility and there may be a lack of trust between members of staff which can prevent a cohesive system of guidance work. It is quite essential that there should be a team approach to the work of guidance in a school or college; without it, counsellors may be ineffectual. When members of staff jeer at the counselling work of a few, then the pupils will sense it and guidance work may fail. Whilst we must accept a variety of viewpoints on guidance work amongst a staff, there must be a professional level of co-operation.

Institutions bring certain ground rules to counselling, and we must assess how far colleagues can be criticised in a counselling situation. Unless there is some element of permitted criticism of an institution and its staff, it is difficult to see how individual and group counselling can be fully effective, for often there will be situations when staff may be criticised for some action. We consider it preferable if no criticism of named colleagues is permitted in group work, and if this is explained as being part of good relationships and fair dealing with other people. Pupils can be very fair in these matters and many will accept that it is a bad example of relationships to criticise those who are not able to defend themselves. Criticism of general attitudes by groups of staff may be permitted in group discussions on relationships, but when criticism of individual teachers arises, it should be explained that these are things which are best discussed between people on an individual basis. In individual counselling such criticism must be acceptable and there must be trust between colleagues that those who counsel in this way are not sitting in judgment on each other, but rather are representing them whilst a problem is ventilated. There will be improvements in relationships if there is honesty in the way that the imperfections of teachers are accepted as part of everyday living.

Parents are often criticised, and again we should avoid allowing pupils to condemn individual parents in group discussion, for this is unkind and often unfair. Professional workers with young people sometimes feel better able to understand the young person than his parents and we may even give parents a feeling that they are hardly qualified to speak on behalf of their own children. One of our pastoral jobs is to see that parents' viewpoints are represented and our role of balancing alternative views must be seen by young people; we are not defending our own age group always, but rather we are balancing how humans look at each other. We must avoid giving an impression that by allowing young people to discuss their family relationships, we are somehow encouraging criticism of parents or inviting parents to opt out of their responsibilities.

It is becoming increasingly important to show young people that apathy and aggression in society are alarming extremes. We may encourage young people to be involved and active in improving the communities they live in. There is then a great problem in how best, especially in counselling through group work, to lead pupils to be critical of what they consider to be evils and inadequacies in society, without giving an impression that we are fostering an anarchical group. Some element of criticism is essential if society is to improve, and angry young people may often rightly wish to break complacency and apathy in authority. How this critical attitude can be encouraged and, at the same time a professional detachment and fairness be maintained, is skilled work. Surely there must be much greater acceptance of risk in the way we encourage pupils to be concerned about the society and community they live in? The temptation is to be orthodox, and to guide young people towards norms which are comfortable. This is hardly likely to change society, and schools and colleges need to review how they can encourage young people to be critical and concerned, and yet to be caring for those who may be upset by changed viewpoints on where society is going.

Problems associated with drugs, alcohol and tobacco

The fields of drugs, alcohol and tobacco are sensitive issues in health and social education at any time; when they are involved with incidents at schools, and pupils require pastoral care and counselling, the degree of sensitivity increases. Unfortunately, some aspects of this field easily arouse fear and emotional responses in those who do the counselling. The management of such incidents may well be beyond the experience of the pastoral staff as, in some cases, only a single incident may arise in a period of several years.

The introduction of this subject demands a wide perspective in order to show how similar are the problems of alcohol, drugs and tobacco to any other type of adolescent problems. There has been a tendency to isolate certain problems of this age group. In the 1960s, there was a considerable emphasis on the taking of various types of illicit drugs by young people, then newspaper coverage declined and the emphasis switched to alcohol, so that public interest became fixed on teenage drinking. Even the slightest knowledge of adolescent psychology would reveal that if one behavioural pattern is attached to an adolescent group, it can quite easily become the norm to which others will conform. It is fairly obvious that the identification of illicit drugs with a teenage culture in the 1960s contributed to the growth of drug-taking among that group.

The difference in ages between counsellor and counselled may cause a second problem when a social problem is related to one age group. It is easy for a barrier to arise between the behaviour of the teachers of one age group and the contrasting behaviour of the adolescent age group. If we talk of illicit drug-taking among young people, the latter then see the older generation as a different culture using different drugs. If teenage drinking is isolated, young people will see adult drinking as different. In order to prevent this categorising of certain problems with adolescents, it is necessary to see the problems in perspective. It is essential that the counsellor should achieve a balanced and unsensational attitude towards the field of chemical use and abuse.

One way of putting alcohol, drug and tobacco problems into perspective is to regard chemically-related problems as being within the context of everyday and domestic chemical use. We live in a society which has a developed technology, and because of this we have developed ways of helping people to live with it; we teach children to take care on the roads and to be careful near machinery; we make people take driving tests and train people to work with machinery. Although we have an advanced chemical technology, we have not yet fully developed ways which will help people to live with it. Educating or counselling about drugs, alcohol and tobacco is one way of achieving this. The counsellor needs to see drugs and alcohol as part of the whole range of chemical use, and this approach should come through to the student. A balanced view is to see that every person has to plan his own chemical career and each person's will be slightly different.

The chemicals with which both counsellor and student come into contact may come from the doctor or over the counter; chemicals stored at home can endanger the lives of children; tobacco and alcohol may be part of their everyday lives; they may experience situations where illicit drugs are used. If we take this broad perspective of drugs, we are better able to put ourselves in the position of the student. No longer is he using a type of drug which the counsellor does not use. No longer need the counsellor feel, 'If I haven't experienced that drug then I can't be of any help'. No longer does he need to think, 'This is all new to me'. The counsellor is in the same position as the student, in that everyone has to plan his use of chemicals and the controls he puts on them. The person being counselled can thus be helped through counselling to plan his use or non-use of chemicals.

Even when a course is run specially to help professional workers acquire a more balanced perspective on drugs, at the end of the course there is always someone who thinks one particular aspect, glue-sniffing for example, is the 'real' problem of the moment. We need to make sure we do not publicise one drug out of perspective. To reiterate, if a satisfactory counselling relationship is to be formed, somehow the barrier has to be crossed and the counsellor must accept that he is part of the same drug-orientated society as the person he is counselling.

Not everyone will want to see alcohol, drugs and tobacco in terms of chemicals. We can also see the use of one or several chemicals as one of many ways of socialising, of coping with stress or of coping with interpersonal relationships.

Chemically-related counselling situations

There is a tendency to consider that a chemically-related situation which requires counselling will also be a crisis one, associated more often with problem pupils than 'normal' ones. This may be because this situation is sensitive and is a feature of counselling that has been neglected. We are often afraid of what we do not understand. In the list that follows we are going to consider the sort of situations requiring counselling help which may occur in a school. This list is not intended to be exhaustive, but may give the reader an idea of how many matters may contain a 'chemical component' which at the very least will need to be recognised, and may need counselling.

(1) A pupil has a parent taking drugs and she has seen a programme on television about people who have become addicted to drugs. She is very worried because she knows her mother constantly takes tablets, and feels the need to tell somebody about it. The mother may, in fact, only be taking tablets prescribed by the doctor, but fear has built up in the girl and it needs ventilating. On the other hand, the mother may be taking large numbers of tablets, which have not been prescribed, in order to cope with stress. In this situation the counsellor acts as a support to the girl while trying to enquire why the mother is acting in this way and whether or not the drugs are prescribed ones.

(2) A pupil is drunk at the school discotheque. He is easily recognised, but the teacher or counsellor has to decide whether or not to take him home and how to help him in the future. It is also necessary to remember that whatever action the counsellor takes will have effects on the pupil's peer group which will also have to be managed.

(3) A pupil is starting to take a number of over-the-counter drugs which are not really needed. Seen today in many schools, this type of student often patterns himself or herself on the mother who has to take something to get through the day.

(4) A pupil is moving into an illicit drug-taking group. The young person may be on the fringe of this group, and meets them only when travelling up to town from a rural area or only at holiday periods. This type of pupil is an excellent case for giving practical guidance.

(5) A pupil is drawn into an illicit drug-taking group. Schools often respond to this in a most unusual and dramatic way, once the pupil's activities are known. They may tolerate half a dozen pregnancies a year, but find one drug-taker far more upsetting.

(6) A pupil has parents who take illicit drugs.

(7) A pupil has a father who is an alcoholic.

(8) A pupil comes from a home where little importance is attached to storing drugs properly.

Chemicals are used in such a variety of contexts that any young person in school may be at risk from some type of chemical at certain ages. It is through education that we may be able to help young people sort out their attitudes and behaviour towards chemicals of all types.

Schools often go to extremes in the policies they adopt in dealing with these types of counselling situations. Often the majority of schools will do nothing until the situation occurs, and then it takes them by surprise. An example of this happens when a very small incident of drug-taking comes to the notice of a school which has not had this type of incident before. As it is outside the staff's experience, they may over-react, as in the following situation.

John and his friends changed the pub they used to frequent and started going to a disco pub in a nearby town, until it became their main meeting place. One night Peter, who was older than John, invited them at 10.30 p.m. to travel to a shebeen in the town. John found the atmosphere of the drinking club exciting, but was uneasy about some of the people there and felt under a very strong pressure not to do anything which might make him stand out. One night he was offered his first smoke of 'pot' there, and accepted it because everyone else did so. On future occasions, John found it difficult to refuse Peter when he rallied them round at the end of an evening at the pub to go to the shebeen, and gradually he found the situation there a little easier. Then the police raided the place and took a group of names, particularly of the younger people there. This information got back to the schools.

Suddenly John's school found that it had a drug-taker in its midst, for so it categorised him, rather than as a young person facing a situation he had not experienced before. The headmaster called him for an interview, and the interviews continued as he was asked to reveal names. The head, harassed by the Press who had now heard about the incident, called the police. They questioned the boy and his friends within the school. The Press decided that this was a major drug incident, and the headlines the next day commented that five or six schools were involved in a drug-taking culture.

Any teacher who was sensitive to the needs of his pupils would say, 'That wouldn't happen in my school. I would deal with it much more calmly.' Certainly some incidents are dealt with calmly, but it is unfortunate that many are inflated out of proportion to the facts.

At the other end of the scale from the 'do nothing until it occurs' schools, are those schools which have a rigid policy. Because of Press sensationalism, a school decides that if drug-taking, drinking or smoking occurs among its pupils, a harsh policy will be followed. This decision is announced to pupils, and letters are sent to parents stating what will happen if the various substances are used by pupils.

Then such an incident does occur; the school finds that the reasons for the pupil finding himself in the situation are quite different from the preconceptions in the minds of the staff when the policy was formulated. However, having set down their plan, the staff have left themselves no room to manoeuvre and find they can only take the action set down in their policy. In calling such a policy an extreme position, we do not wish to suggest that schools should not have rules on these subjects; rather we would suggest that care must be taken to ensure that these rules do not confine the staff, and in particular the pastoral care team.

In a school with a rigid policy it is also more likely that children will find sophisticated ways of covering up their behaviour for fear of being caught. Will a more relaxed approach make it easier for pupils to go to staff with problems of this kind if they are unafraid of immediate punitive reprisals?

What is obviously needed is a middle way between the school with no policy and the school with a policy which is too rigid. The following is meant as a pointer to this middle position.

(1) It is essential that methods of coping with such situations are discussed by the head teacher and his administrative team and the pastoral staff before they actually occur. In a school with a developed awareness of pastoral responsibility, the whole staff might even attend. The guidelines need to be reviewed as the staff team changes, so that once the policy has been decided, it cannot be forgotten. Discussions before incidents occur are possibly the most important factor in the management of sensitive situations.

(2) The policy agreed upon should not be announced to the school in the form of a decree about acceptable behaviour. The discussion will be for the guidance of the staff only, so that they know where they stand if presented with an incident.

(3) If the following themes have not been discussed in relation to pastoral care, then the staff group needs to discuss them.
(a) What are the guidelines on confidentiality?
(b) At what stage should the head teacher be brought in?
(c) At what stage, if any, should parents be brought in?
(d) What type of pastoral training is needed for the teachers most likely to have to deal with these types of incidents?
(e) At what stage does the school turn to outside agencies?
(f) What complementary education could be given as a preventive step?

(4) Structured education on these subjects can be of considerable help, if it is complementary to the counselling which is taking place and not the other way round. In many schools education about alcohol and drugs exists, but no facilities exist for pupils to discuss their personal attitudes and problems on the subject. They may go to a class tutor to discuss what they heard in biology or social studies and find him unhelpful simply because he has never thought constructively about the subject.

(5) The group then needs to apply their own conclusions on these issues to a number of the types of drug situations which may occur in schools. Some of the complexities which arise in the managements of these situations are discussed in the following sections.

(Appendix E lists many questions which staff may wish to discuss in in-service work in schools and colleges, and Appendix F gives an example of the advice an LEA may offer to schools.)

Confidentiality

To what extent is a counsellor solely responsible to his client? There must obviously be trust between the young person and the counsellor, for the youngster will not, in fact, talk to those whom he does not trust to have a sense of privacy, yet personal counselling will often bring information to light which can be very grave and which can have an effect on others. A dramatic example could be that of incest. Teachers frequently hear of cases of minor criminal offences and of incidents of drug misuse.

A counsellor will possibly feel compelled to inform others in order to help a young person, but if this is done without consent it may destroy the relationship. The problem may be to know whether we have a prior duty to inform a head teacher, a loyalty to an institution of which we are very obvious members, or whether we should in fact inform the police or other agencies in order to help the individual or to safeguard others. Since there is no clear legal status for counsellors, it is essential that those who counsel at any depth are people of sensitivity and wisdom, for they must take personal decisions on confidentiality.

The law is not easy to summarise in this matter but the following points can be considered.

(1) Doctors hold no legal privilege to refuse evidence if a patient faces criminal legal proceedings and priests hold no specific privilege of confidentiality in law. Journalists and accountants have had claims for privilege disallowed.

(2) Section 4 of the Criminal Law Act of 1967 makes it an offence to impede the apprehension or prosecution of arrestable offenders by the police, but the counsellor appears to have no obligation to report information to them provided that he has not benefitted in any way. Non-arrestable offences require no obligation to inform or assist the police, though in a trial it might be contempt to refuse evidence in court.

(3) A counsellor must not, of course, give assistance or encouragement for a crime, but is not necessarily guilty at law in knowing of a crime or even of being present at the scene of a crime and doing nothing to prevent it.

(4) Providing the student has not requested that his parents be informed of his problem, there seems no duty on the part of a teacher-counsellor to disclose to anyone else the problem revealed by a pupil aged under sixteen. A teacher is deemed to have good sense in the professional task of helping and advising a youngster. His competence in counselling would be judged on whether he acted in a manner consistent with professional standards that the circumstances demand.

(Appendix D adds further information on legal matters.)

The counsellor, therefore, has ill-defined and limited legal protection in considering confidentiality in criminal matters and there cannot be an easy set of rules. Usually it is possible to get the agreement of a young person to refer matters elsewhere—in fact, thankfully, this is almost invariably the case. However, when this permission is refused, only the maturity of the counsellor can help in deciding whether the confidentiality is to be broken or not.

In a school which has a clear pastoral policy and with a well-organised pastoral staff, the head teacher may well pass the responsibility for making counselling and confidentiality decisions to staff members. He will accept that information gained in counselling need not always be passed on to him in detail. Most head teachers are able to trust selected members of staff with such a role of safeguarding confidential matters, knowing that they will be warned of the essential matters. Many head teachers rightly feel that they need to know about incidents which have legal implications. The teacher who is dealing with counselling cases will need then to help the young person to understand that the school authorities have to be informed, though perhaps names may be withheld for a time. The teacher may then let the pupil know when a stage has been reached when names and information have to be passed on. If the young person will not reveal information because the teacher will have to tell others, the teacher can perhaps help the pupil to see someone, such as a youth worker, who is not in the institutional setting. Where the head teacher feels he needs to know full details about all major counselling incidents, the staff have to trust the head teacher's integrity and reassure the youngster of that. The head teacher should make sure that his pastoral staff know he will not over-react and will discuss cases with them carefully.

Schools must recognise the vital importance of this mutual confidence. A head of year in a school known to us, furious over his head teacher's decision to call in the parents of children who had not returned to school after lunchtime drinking, felt that the school could have handled this by discussion and support of the children. The head teacher felt it was solely a discipline matter and the staff were divided on the issue. One suspects no-one was to blame, but the systems had failed to recognise the need for mutual confidence and for discussing ways of handling such incidents before they arise.

Parental involvement

Parents are naturally the people who should be closest to the child, and the school has a distinct responsibility to them. It is possible, however, that due to lack of tact or wisdom, parents can be brought in at the wrong time and without the young person's consent. In this sort of situation the school has a real dilemma. On the one hand, if parents are not brought in and the problem gets worse despite counselling, when the parents do learn of their child's problem they have every right to complain. On the other hand, it may seem to a pupil that bringing in parents is betraying his confidence in the counsellor. One possible solution to the dilemma is the attitude taken by the Venereal Disease Clinics. These encourage young people to discuss the problem with their parents, but leave the decision to the young person. Schools are obviously in a different position from such clinics, but many counsellors feel it is an essential preliminary always to encourage children to discuss problems with their parents. In other cases, the counsellor may have to tell the parents himself. Sometimes a youngster agrees to have someone who will represent him to his parents, for he fears to do so himself; and sometimes the counsellor decides that the parents are the best people to help a young person in a particular case. Sometimes, also, a teacher or counsellor sees with a sense of desperation that he has reached the limit of his competence and, after consulting with colleagues, passes a problem back to the parents, even when a young person argues to the contrary. This is when we may have failed and when the family has to deal with its own problem; even then we must leave a lifeline by offering support for the parents or referring them to a social agency.

A different problem arises when parents are the main reason for the problem. Let us take the case of Mary. She was on the outskirts of a drug-taking group, so the school referred the matter to her parents. They immediately took her to the doctor, who sent her to a psychiatrist, and she finished in the Drug Dependency ward of an Adolescent Unit. She came out of the unit knowing all the terms for drugs and places to obtain them. Had there not been over-reaction in this way it is possible that Mary would simply have grown out of an adolescent phase. This is not an isolated case. One often finds that people have chemically-related problems owing to their inability to relate to others without chemical aids. When the problem is traced back to its roots, very often the cause is found in the home.

In many cases the good counsellor should be able to re-establish the lines of communication between parent and child by continued support, and discussion with the parents at a suitable time, for we cannot, of course, ignore or sidetrack the parents' responsibility. When parents are a contributory factor to a pupil's problem, helpful advice must first be given to the young person. It may be possible to increase understanding of the pressures the parents are under; it may be possible to make him aware of areas between him and his parents which are not points of conflict; it may be possible to increase the young person's sensitivity; or it may, in fact, be necessary to help him simply to accept the situation. Counsellors sometimes try to change situations for their clients rather than helping them develop ways of coping with the stress inherent in the situation, yet helping people to cope with facts may, in the end, be a far more mature method.

If we visit parents, or invite them to meet us in order to discuss their child, we will meet a variety of reactions. These will range from the concerned attitude, through the 'I'll knock the living daylights out of him' type attitude, to the 'couldn't care less' one. Some parents, faced with sensitive issues such as drugs and alcohol, will consider the situation and work through it with their child. The parent who over-reacts will be calmed by the good counsellor and helped to see that he needs to stand by his child and try to understand his problem. The parent will need to try to build up communication again. The counsellor has to be careful that in the ensuing weeks he does not only give support to the young person— that is often the easier part. It is easy to forget that the parents also will need continuing support, as they come to appreciate the situation and perhaps constantly bring it up with their child. The good counsellor will try to keep in contact with the parents and give them adequate support.

Schools have developed many different methods of trying to involve parents in all they do, including the impression that the school guidance is a joint effort with the parents. Apart from general and repeated invitations to discuss their children with staff, a regular pattern of 'open days' and 'curriculum explanation' sessions are held. Senior staff may have regular advertised sessions when it is known that they are available for interview or discussion with groups of parents. One very successful comprehensive high school has developed a regular 'family evening' when a variety of sports and activities take place, with ample opportunities for informal contacts and conversations with staff. The same school has its heads of departments describing their work, including their pastoral responsibilities, to governors' meetings and to packed parents' meetings, the most popular of which has been when the school's programme of education in personal relationships and tutorial work is explained and discussed. For trust and co-operation to develop fully we have to be available and vulnerable to parents' demanding questions and comments—in that way we illustrate our professional confidence and competence. And in the long run it makes a difficult job easier, perhaps!

Outside agencies

There has been a tendency for teachers to turn to outside agencies when they are presented with situations of which they have had little experience. It is to be hoped that teachers will come to understand better the concept of giving help to people so that they may develop a healthy use of chemicals, rather than just giving help when crises occur, in order that teachers will realise that chemically-related problems are little different from other adolescent problems. It is, of course, in no way 'wrong' for the teacher-counsellor to admit to the youngster seeking his help, 'As I haven't experienced what you are going through, let me try to find you someone who can advise you on that particular aspect, and we can go further once you feel that aspect is being sorted out.' It is, however, essential that if the counsellor feels the need to get outside help, he should know the skills and reactions of the outside body, and that he has discussed the outside help with the youngster first.

The abilities and attitudes of outside agencies vary. Some who should know about such subjects as drugs and alcohol do not; some over-react; some refuse to work closely with the teacher using the approaches he has been using; some are paternal; some are very good. In order to manage this aspect of counselling, the school should have sounded out members of these outside agencies so that, knowing their reactions, the school can build relationships with those who are sympathetic to the school's approach and forget the unhelpful ones. In some areas, lunchtime meetings are developing between the school and social workers, probation officers, ministers, youth workers, and other professionals, Some of these meetings, often held monthly, stagnate as they accomplish little more than nominal liaison. Others progress when they are properly planned, choosing topics to be discussed, having an input of information, and then discussing the contributions that different professions can make in a particular situation. This development is very helpful, as counsellors can become far more effective if they know of the potential available from others.

When considering outside agencies, it is important to stress the importance of the teacher-counsellor ensuring that the few pupils who have very deep problems are referred to outside help. The school should be a place where most children are normal and where normal problems can be alleviated, but the school also sieves problems, working with other professionals, who can take over the guidance when required. School counsellors are not amateur psychiatrists, but they must be sufficiently aware of the signs of stress and the signs of mental illness to know when problems should be referred. Earlier diagnosis and earlier treatment of deeper emotional problems could bring earlier alleviation.

The following agencies and individuals may offer help in referral of cases which the school cannot deal with.

(1) *Statutory Agencies:*
Educational psychologists
Medical officers and school nurses
Social Service staff
Probation Service
Police, especially Juvenile Liaison Officers
Educational Welfare Officers
Special School and Remedial Centre staff
Housing Department staff
LEA Advisors
Health Education Officers
Career Service staff
(2) *Voluntary agencies and individuals:*
General practitioners and Health Visitors
National Marriage Guidance Council Counsellors
Catholic Marriage Guidance Council Counsellors
Councils for Social (or Voluntary) Service
Citizens Advice Bureaux
Diocesan Councils for Social Work
Councils for Alcohol and Drug Dependence

NSPCC
Samaritans
Local Councillors
Young People's Advisory Centres
Counsellors in local colleges and universities
Employers
Clergy

Prescribed and over-the-counter drugs

If a problem comes to light, often in the course of discussing a completely different issue, the counsellor can find himself in a difficult position between the patient and the doctor. It could, for example, be noticed that a child is always sleepy in school, and through discussion it emerges that he has been on tranquillisers for some time. Should the teacher-counsellor advise the child to talk it over with the doctor? The next time the parents visit the school should they be asked to discuss it with the doctor? Should the teacher probe delicately to find out why the child is taking these prescribed drugs? Is there something, such as the death of a relative, which has seriously disturbed the young person? Is the mother over-reacting to this situation by not allowing either herself or the child to face up to it? Or, in fact, has the child every good reason for being on tranquillisers and is he possibly being unnecessarily worried about this by the teacher? All of these need tactfully looking into and the most useful course of action needs deciding.

There is, unfortunately, a tendency to over-react on the subject of drugs, so that they are seen as all bad or all good. The counsellor needs to be sensitive to the reasons why one particular person may be taking them. As we have stated before, a good counsellor needs to be able to see a situation through the young person's eyes.

Aspirin is easily available in many schools and teachers rarely use a request for an aspirin as a pick-up point for pastoral care. Some pupils no doubt ask because they are copying their mothers who take something to get through the day; some don't like geography; some ask to get attention; some find the school secretary who gives out the aspirin a good friend, good-looking or even possibly a good counsellor. Pastoral staff need to be aware of these situations so that the knowledge can be of use to them. The reasons behind such requests need to be analysed.

The overdose, of course, is a worrying type of incident. Overdoses seem to be happening more frequently among adolescents, and are clearly cries for help. The teacher needs to ask where the drugs came from, and examine the possibility of the removal of such temptation. Obviously the pupil who takes an overdose is in need of continuing counselling and help. The teacher will need to find out at some stage how serious the overdose was and whether it was accidental or suicidal. He may need to seek specialist help concerning for instance suicidal overdoses. Sometimes the member of staff who could help never hears of the incident, as such information may remain at one level of school administration.

Smoking

Most schools have rules about smoking, but it is important in terms of how the school can cope with incidents that such rules are regularly discussed. Variations between schools and colleges are considerable; some ban it altogether, while some may have rooms for smokers.

The main difficulty which arises in this issue is that pupils quickly recognise the difference in expected standards between them and the teachers and society in general. It must be remembered also that some young people are addicted to tobacco, so it may be unrealistic to expect them to go without a cigarette for a whole day. This situation needs to be talked through as carefully as possible so that the position finally reached is at least not incongruous, for a perfect solution and a perfect set of rules is not possible. Support or facilities need to be planned for pupils who wish to give up smoking, and—less recognised these days—for those who wish to cut down the number of cigarettes they smoke.

It is interesting to check how many children of particular age groups do smoke. In a survey in one East Lancashire secondary school, a sample of pupils aged fifteen to sixteen answered part of a written questionnaire as follows.

Q. Do you smoke	*Result*
More than 10 a day?	19
5–10 a day?	19
Less than five a day?	12
At odd times?	43
Never smoke?	146

We can sometimes overestimate a problem, perhaps, by viewing only the active minority.

Alcohol

As with smoking, the problems which alcohol causes are mostly in terms of the ability of the teacher to cope with a pupil or group of pupils and the question of school rules. The legal position, that only people over eighteen are allowed to *purchase* alcohol, means that the large majority of young people in schools are below the legal age limit. The legal situation is therefore similar to that of illicit drugs, but few people see it in the same way.

The school pastoral staff need to discuss their aims. If it is to stop or discourage under-age drinkers, then their goal in counselling will be fairly directive. If the aim is to minimise the consequences, accepting that many young people do drink under-age, then the staff will start with the drinking the child is already doing and help him to achieve safer controls on his habit. If the aim is not discussed it will cause confusion, preventing meaningful relationships in counselling. After deciding aims, the staff will then need to discuss the action to be taken over various incidents. If a young person comes in drunk, what will be done? Will the school punish him? How will it find out where he got drunk? Will it enquire why the person came into school? The hysteria that was once seen over illicit drugs is now being seen over young people's drinking. If the situations are talked through thoroughly in advance, the incidents will not then be exaggerated.

Another perspective to be considered on such issues is the question, 'Who matters most?' Sometimes the important factor is the reputation of the school; sometimes it is the effect on other pupils; sometimes the pupil needs to be safeguarded. What, then, will be the position of the school? Many schools will feel that it is far better to take a low-key counselling approach and give practical help in sobering the young person up, sending him home and then giving him the opportunity to discuss the problem with someone he trusts. This approach may lead to less publicity and more realistic help for the child.

Illicit drugs

Many teachers can come to terms with all the topics so far mentioned, but the very words 'illicit drugs' will cause cries of 'Get them out of school!' and 'They should have had the willpower to say no!' These reactions may be due to the fantasies of high-powered 'pushers' and the tales once told of the likelihood of half-a-million addicts by 1980. All the evidence shows that illicit drug-taking still goes on, that the numbers of drug-takers are not rising astronomically, but also that only those who have no experience of drug-takers would say that it is likely to die out. Any young person may start to take illicit drugs, for any young person, of whatever background, intelligence or race, may find himself in a situation where illicit drugs are available.

Schools usually want to know how they can recognise a young person taking illicit drugs. Even those who have spent a considerable part of their working lives with drug-takers would admit that they could not recognise even a heavy experimenter unless he was under the influence at the time they saw him. On odd occasions, a young person may be unsophisticated enough to let traces of drugs be found, but it is probable that the amount of drugs supposedly consumed by schoolchildren in the 1960s was grossly exaggerated. Most young people (who eventually use drugs) start experimenting either right at the end of their school careers, or just after they have left school. The most irrelevant details have been published on supposed guidelines for recognising drug-takers, the size of the pupil of the eye being one of the most frequent. Extended pupils are only seen acutely in addicts and addiction takes a long time to build up, by which time even the most naive teacher ought to know that something was wrong. Mood changes were another favourite, but anyone working with adolescents knows the extent of their mood changes. In some cases it is possible that mood changes can be taken as non-verbal communication to the counsellor that further enquiries need to be made, but that is the extent of their use as a sign.

The majority of cases that come to the counsellor's attention in schools are those where a pupil has come with one problem which appears to have no connection with drugs, but in the course of conversation the pupil reveals that he has been moving in drug-taking circles, either on the edge or fully involved. The school then has a dilemma: it may want to help the young person, but fears that other pupils may be affected by him; the school may also possibly feel that the young person has information useful to the police. The facts of the matter, however, may put the case in a different light; if a pupil has revealed that he takes drugs, it is very unlikely that he will attempt to interest others in the school; also his contacts for drugs will most likely not be in school, but be in an outside group. A school with a well-defined counselling system with determined bounds of confidentiality will not experience as many problems over this type of incident as a less prepared school.

There are many different ways schools can handle such incidents. Some schools decide that in the case of illicit drugs being used the police need to be involved at an early stage and they should handle the incident. Other schools use methods similar to those outlined below. (1) An automatic reaction to call in the drug squad, psychological service or local social worker may be delayed. In some areas the police are very willing to advise and come in at the invitation of the head teacher and on the head teacher's terms. In other areas, unfortunately, the police do not respect the wishes of the head teacher on the handling of the incident, and in some cases where the police have been involved the Press seems to hear of the incidents too quickly.

It is therefore essential that the head teacher or education advisers know how the local drug squad function and checks any changes if a new senior officer takes over the squad. One officer may differ greatly from another as regards his approach. It may be more appropriate to call in the Police Juvenile Liaison Officers, as these may be more sympathetic in their approach to young people and to schools. We have found the police to be exceptionally helpful in the majority of cases and very open to considering ways in which they can liaise with schools. It is well worthwhile for schools to make contact with the police prior to these sorts of incidents occurring, so that police and teachers can get to know each other and work our the most appropriate way in one locality for an incident to be handled. There are a growing number of police who recognise the confidentiality which teachers and head teachers expect within those schools which have a good pastoral care system.

There has not been a test case concerning counsellors and drugs, so one can only go by the letter of the law. According to the Misuse of Drugs Act 1973, a person is allowed to remove drugs from a user, provided he intends to hand them to a police officer or destroy them. The latter is naturally taken to assume that some people, such as counsellors, will be in the position to destroy drugs, in order to avoid breaking the confidence of the person being counselled. The clause is therefore of obvious use to the counsellor in allowing confidentiality at his own discretion and should therefore placate concern over the legal aspects.

(2) The teacher who learns of a young person's drug-taking should convince him that he can discuss it without action being taken at that stage. There is, however, every reason for the teacher to state clearly the legal consequence of drug-taking, as a combination of hard and soft approaches is necessary. The counselling can continue, but the pupil needs to realise that he is breaking the law and that police action could be taken. In some schools this approach is developed so that, after prior discussion with his staff about the handling of such incidents, the head teacher sees the pupil and takes a firm line, stating that he will be monitoring whether other pupils are being affected, and at the same time the counsellor provides continued support for the young person. The nature of this support will be discussed later.

(3) The teacher, head teacher and anyone else involved then monitor the development of the child. It may be reasonable to bring in an outside agency once the situation has been analysed. It may also be possible to let the young person give information to the police, either directly or through an intermediary, once his confidence has been gained and his agreement reached. This freely given information may be more realistic in aim than the little snippets squeezed out of the student by force, which leads to a subsequent bad relationship between young people and the police.

Some schools still feel that removal is the best policy. Experience has shown that the following is likely to occur if a child is severely punished or removed. Firstly, if a pupil is moved to another school, the aura which can build up around him may influence other pupils there. Secondly, a pupil isolated in this manner is thrown back on the drug-taking group as being the only people with whom he feels secure. Thirdly, the school imagines that the problem has gone away, yet often peers copy the same behaviour about six months later, but are sufficiently sophisticated to make sure that the school does not find out. Finally, if there exists one such topic which pupils feel unable to discuss with staff then there may be more and it is a poor prospect for pastoral care and learning.

The procedure in (2) and (3) above is recommended in schools where the pupil is prepared to discuss his drug-taking, but it is not suitable for the delinquent adolescent who is hitting out at the school in every way, drug-taking being only one symptom of his view of authority. This type of help is not going to stop him influencing others. In many cases the delinquent adolescent does not start taking drugs until he has tried most other forms of behaviour, and drug-taking is not likely to occur until late in his school career. Few start taking drugs during their earlier school years.

The following sane advice was given in a DES publication on drugs and the schools: 'There is much to be said for a cooling off period, for keeping a sense of proportion, and for knowing when to seek expert help'. It goes on to say; 'If there is reason to suppose that several members of a school are involved in drug-taking the possibility that their source of supplies may be one of the children or some person . . . in the vicinity of the school cannot be ignored.'

In such cases teachers must, for obvious reasons consider whether the police should be advised at an early stage.

7

Individuals and their problems

So far we have looked at general ideas on how staff can cope with situations within the school context, but now we have to ask how the person developing the counselling relationships actually gives some help. The purpose of this chapter is to consider some of the practical aspects of counselling within these aspects of human behaviour.

Alcohol-related problems

The counsellor has a student who is drinking in a way apparently unhelpful to himself. The first question the counsellor must ask himself is, 'Do I want to stop him drinking, or am I going to attempt to help him re-evaluate his drinking habits so as to lower the consequences of his drinking?' If the former is the counsellor's aim, probably because the student is under-age, then this responsibility is not really the job of the counsellor, but of the school, which will be concerned with aspects of discipline. In terms of counselling it is much more likely that the latter question should be the one dealt with, so that the young person can be helped to understand what is happening to him in terms of his drinking habits.

It is useful to analyse carefully with a young person what the actual factor is which is worrying him about his drinking, or what the counsellor can see might be a factor in other future problems. To talk about drinking in general terms is of little use, because the young person will probably see his drinking simply in terms of behaviour learned from parents or friends and will not be able to see that his personal behaviour is different from theirs. There are a number of attitudes which can be considered. It has already been suggested that any counselling needs to start non-directively, but as there exists an ambivalence of attitudes and a lack of understanding about alcohol, there is probably a need to put forward a number of suggestions for the young person to consider.

One of the most important aspects is that most young people do not appreciate that alcohol is a depressant. Many may know that it is called a depressant, but compared to their perception of how it acts upon them arising from their experience of drinking, this will have little real meaning.

A counsellor may, for instance, have before him a student who is going through a stage of getting intoxicated on a number of occasions, and who seems to be unable to curb his behaviour. The first possibility to be considered is that the young person wants to be intoxicated. This cannot be ignored, and if the student is happy with his drinking behaviour, the counsellor may need to move on to other subjects of discussion and leave this aspect for a time. Alternatively, it may well be that drunkenness is a symptom of other feelings, such as boredom, frustration and the desire for an euphoric experience, and that these feelings will have to be explored.

The second possibility is that the young person does not understand the effects of alcohol. If this is so, the counsellor will first need to discuss with the student his perception of what alcohol does to him. Should the reply be that alcohol stimulated him, the counsellor can then explain alcohol's effect in making the brain less competent in its reasoning and judgement.

Many young people drink through an evening at the discotheque, having previously been to a pub. They limit their drinking at each place, but have no idea that alcohol remains in the body from the previous drinking session. Thus they build up a high intake of alcohol, without seeing it as such.

'A student, Dave, was giving me a lift in his car, and as he drove along he told me that he had just finished off three pints, and that was all he had been drinking. At this stage I began to feel a little uneasy. Then he talked of the two pints he drank at lunchtime with friends and the three pints of canned beer he consumed after that at a friend's house. At this stage I began to contemplate how I could get out of the car! Yet he had initially talked of having "only three pints" because he thought of consumption only in terms of what he had last drunk.'

Many young people do not realise the length of time that alcohol is active in the body—one pint of beer or two martinis affects us for three hours, so four pints affects us for nearly twelve hours. The fact that the high peak of blood alcohol content is not reached immediately is also not properly understood. Young people will often talk of feeling more intoxicated when they have stopped drinking for a while or gone outside. The effects of oxygen on the bloodstream can also cause this, but mostly it is due to the length of time it takes alcohol to reach its maximum content in the blood. The counsellor will need to explain this to such people as Peter, for example, who drives a scooter; having decided to set his limits at two pints, he then goes over the limit and so decides to wait before he drives home. When he does finally go, however, he is more affected by the alcohol than ever, because of the length of time it takes alcohol to reach its high peak of content in the blood.

Practical safety measures are an important part of this type of counselling. Stuart has a weekend job after school with machinery on a farm. He goes out drinking in the lunch hour with the older workers. One of the factors the counsellor must discuss is what measures can be taken to ensure safety. He may be able to discuss appropriate and inappropriate drinking styles. Looking at 'safety' in a different light, Pamela cannot understand why it is that although she always sets her limits at three martinis, she gets drunk at a party but never at a pub or disco. Here the counsellor needs to explain how glasses are much fuller at parties, so she is drinking more actual alcohol without realising it.

The counsellor can slowly help his student to discuss the rules he can apply to his drinking. A wide range of rules can be suggested as they become relevant and the young person helped to decide how they can be applied. If the person is already drinking, then the rules he chooses will be to lessen the depressant effect of alcohol as far as possible, to prevent accidents and to prevent unpleasant effects. A considerable number of cases of drunkenness amongst young people are probably due to the fact that they do not appreciate fully the strength and effects of the alcohol in the drinks they are using.

The behavioural effect of alcohol is another aspect which needs to be considered. Most young people are slightly affected in their behaviour by alcohol, but some people change more radically; it has been suggested that adolescents are among those most at risk of radical effects upon their behaviour by using alcohol. They may have a greater tendency towards aggression whilst under the influence and a greater tencency to act out their emotions more strongly in certain situations. This is due to inhibitions being depressed by the alcohol, combined with the natural energy of youth. An obvious example is the behaviour of young football supporters who may drink, at the pubs on the way to the ground and then become aggressive. In counselling, we must be careful that we do not ascribe behaviour to a supposed cause rather than the true one. Alcohol may cause aggressive behaviour, but it may also be that a person is naturally aggressive, or that a person works out an expected group behaviour which is repeated week after week.

If after talking to the student, the counsellor finds that alcohol is partly the cause of anti-social behaviour, then he must start to encourage the young person to consider if there are ways he could minimise the amount of aggression he feels. This is a difficult area, for the counsellor may well find that the young person is unable to change a routine he is accustomed to, and cannot suggest an alternative because he has not experienced any. This may be a case where the counsellor has to move to a more directive approach suggesting different strategies for changing this situation, such as meeting the group at the gates of the football ground, coming out with less money, or possibly if the group consists of a number of smaller sub-groups, attaching himself more strongly to one of the other sub-groups who do not seem to get so heavily involved in the drinking and anti-social behaviour. The counsellor may find that it is the whole group which he has to work with rather than just the individual.

Counselling in the situation where problem behaviour is already recognised is relatively easy. As the counsellor helps a young person to think about his drinking he may need to recognise that the student may have other behavioural changes through drinking, which may occur in the future due to emotional immaturity or instability. This is only a possibility not a certainty, for it is impossible to predict how alcohol affects people in certain emotional states in certain situations. The counsellor can ensure that the doors are left open for the person to come and talk further at a later date.

A considerable amount of crime is associated with alcohol. The Helping Hand Organisation suggests that at least half of Britain's prisoners are in jail because of drinking problems, and other statistics quote higher proportions. Borstals, too, are increasingly aware of the number of inmates who have a drink problem and a large number of prisoners have a high chance of a drink problem when release occurs. It is strange that, in the course of counselling disturbed children or those who have started on minor crimes, enquiries are rarely made into the childrens' drinking habits. If these enquiries were made and preventive counselling offered, the number of juveniles appearing before the courts might be reduced. Young people do not conceptualise, or if they do, do not take it seriously, the effect that alcohol has on their behaviour—'I got up and said that I'd thump him one. When I think now, he was bigger than me!' Only after working through every step of what happened with this young person did he begin to accept that this was not the way that he would normally act. With no drink inside him he would have sat still, said nothing and at the earliest opportunity got out as quickly as possible!

The counsellor may come across young people in the course of his work who seem to be in a high-risk group for alcoholism or drinking problems. Young people do not visualise their own drinking as being in any way connected with alcoholism. It may be as well to talk to them about the possibility of this occurring, if signs are present indicating that the person is in a high-risk group. The important factor in considering whether a person is likely to become alcoholic is to understand the stages by which alcoholism develops.

There are two early stages which are possible preludes to a drinking style which may be one leading to alcoholism. The first one is simply drinking to excess regularly. We are very unlikely to find that schoolchildren have reached this level of intake of alcohol except for the very rare case or in certain communities. The amount often given as a danger sign that the person may be moving into a high-risk group for harm from their drinking is five pints of beer daily. Some epidemiological studies* suggest that beyond this point many people will be in high-risk groups. What is important to remember, however is that a person may be drinking below this amount, yet still be in a high-risk group for his particular personality. Such a case might be an adolescent who seems to have developed a need for drinking quite a number of glasses a day. It is possible that this is situationally induced, and in our discussion with him we may find it necessary to discuss this as a preventive measure. The counsellor with a high regard for health may find it difficult at this point to be non-directive. It is essential to recognise that the factors which cause such drinking may be far more important to the young person than the health factors mitigating against such behaviour. The position of importance which we give to health in our criteria of behaviour may be very different from that given it by the student.

A second early stage is drinking to alleviate tension. In a society where, if more people are not actually suffering from tension than before, they are at least more aware of stress, it is natural that alcohol will be used to suppress anxiety. Alcohol can cause dependence and there seems to be a tendency for some young people to drink alcohol for its drug effect when becoming euphoric or intoxicated, rather than drinking it for enjoyment and slight relaxation. If the counsellor finds that his student is drinking in this way, then he is dealing with a person who is in a high-risk group for becoming alcoholic. It is necessary to analyse carefully the reasons for the client drinking in this way, being careful that the situation is seen through the young person's eyes—the drinking may just be due to the group he goes around with. If the client is not happy with the fact that he drinks to alleviate tension in the group and to bolster himself up, then the counsellor can look with him at the situations where he is tense.

Philip, for example, was a classic case of social isolation. He was exceptionally tense in his relationships with other people, feeling awkward when he was invited along to the pub by his friends. Once he was aware of his problem in relating he thought about it more and more, and less and less about anything else. As he thought less about general things, he had less to talk about in the group, so he felt even more uneasy, thought even more about his problems and his social isolation started to cut deeply into his personality. Philip started to drink before he actually met the group in order to be uninhibited in

---

* 'Current trends in the prevalence of excessive alcohol use and alcohol related health damage', J. De Lint, *Br. J. Addiction* (Longman), 1975, Vol. 70, pp. 3–13.

their presence. By doing so he increased his social isolation, but the group did notice him when he behaved in this manner, and that acted as a motive. By careful counselling, Philip could have been encouraged to replan various aspects of the way in which he socialised. Firstly, he could have been encouraged to meet one friend before going to the pub so that it was not so difficult to enter the group. Secondly, he could have had some help on how to relate to other people, what to talk about and how to express himself.

Other young people may just be worried about their personal circumstances and find that drinking blots them out. Stephanie felt that nobody really bothered about her. She had friends, but felt that they did not really care and, as one of a large family, little attention was paid to her at home. These ideas, her fears and her loneliness became too much to cope with; when she was in a group drinking these fears were blotted out in euphoria. In such a situation, the counsellor needs to be very wise. If he concentrates too much on the drinking, he may help the young person to see it as a way out of a crisis. If he ignores it, he may leave the young person unaware of the effects of heavy drinking and in danger of becoming alcoholic. Considerable time, therefore, needs to be spent on the human factors, the reasons for the person's drinking, rather than concentrating just on the drinking by itself.

The good counsellor will be very sensitive over the terminology that they use. For some people (rarely those of school or college age) who are exhibiting serious symptoms of harm due to drinking, it may be easier to conceptualise their behaviour in terms of alcoholism. For the majority of late teens and young adults, this term will not help them and talking about their style of drinking and possible harm coming from it may be more productive.

Alcohol abuse can show itself by producing harm in a person's social life or in their health. Young people may pass in and out of harm, and some, because of their personalities or circumstances, will become dependent on alcohol.

Harm:

(1) difficulties with friends, relatives, or colleagues (disagreements, fights, violence, separation, money troubles, late or absent from work or studies because of alcohol);
(2) accidents;
(3) health (more vulnerable to ulcers, cirrhosis, heart disease, and also to problems associated with inadequate diet).

Dependence

Not everyone will enter dependence in the same way, but the following chart gives two general patterns which often occur.

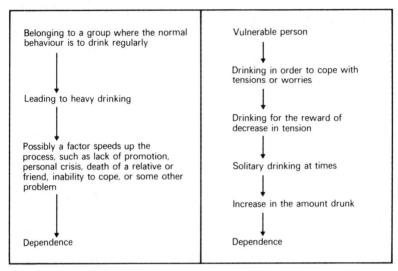

Belonging to a group where the normal behaviour is to drink regularly

↓

Leading to heavy drinking

↓

Possibly a factor speeds up the process, such as lack of promotion, personal crisis, death of a relative or friend, inability to cope, or some other problem

↓

Dependence

Vulnerable person

↓

Drinking in order to cope with tensions or worries

↓

Drinking for the reward of decrease in tension

↓

Solitary drinking at times

↓

Increase in the amount drunk

↓

Dependence

[Reprinted from "Guidelines for Parents", TACADE, 1977, by permission of TACADE.]

It is important that with young people we should differentiate between drunkenness and alcoholism. Drunkenness has its own short-term problems, for instance, a hangover or an accident. Alcoholism is progressive and longer term.

Danger signs:

(1) if a child drinks secretly;
(2) if they bolster themselves up to meet others;
(3) if they become drunk regularly;
(4) if they drink large amounts without getting drunk;
(5) if they drink when tense;
(6) if they drink when alone;
(7) if blackouts occur.

Supporting the individual in the group

We can often be drawn into supporting and counselling those involved in behaviour leading to ill-health, but fail to give sufficient attention to those who find it difficult to stick to the type of behaviour they have already decided upon. In a school or youth club, for example, there may be a young man who does not drink alcohol and is perfectly balanced and happy. In the youth club, however, there is a bar, and he feels great pressure being exerted on him to conform to the group norm of drinking. This type of person needs support and help to be able to keep to his decision, without becoming excessively ill at ease in the group setting. The youth club leader can give support by drinking soft drinks in the bar himself sometimes, such as when he has to drive, so as to show the young people that there are valid reasons for not drinking alcohol at times and to prove that the alternatives to alcohol can be equally attractive.

With regret, we doubt if earlier teaching about personal decisions will have a profound effect on a young person's choice of action at a particular moment in an evening out with a lively and established group of friends. If the pressures of a group of friends are concerted and demanding, perhaps in some question of drinking or smoking, then it takes a strong personality to stand out against them. However, the effect of such group pressures can at least be fully understood and discussed during schooling and, perhaps with a knowledge of facts about alcohol and smoking and with discussion about social and decision-making tactics, there may be some help for a youngster in a group.

Drinking habits of parents

One can find young people who are being emotionally affected by the drinking habits or alcoholism of their parents. Little can be done actually to change the home situation, but the support given by the counsellor to the pupil can enable him to understand this behaviour and the reasons for it and can prove invaluable. Some young people develop a considerable ability to cope, while others just build up the ability to appear to cope—the scars are not seen on the surface until many years later. The counsellor needs to be able to distinguish between the pupil who is coping and who is determined to carry on doing so, and the pupil who is being pulled apart by the situation at home. For the former, support should continue; for the latter, continuing counselling and help will be needed.

It is essential that teachers should not write off the child from a difficult home. We often conceptualise the child from such a home at an early stage in a different way. We suggest when we discuss the pupil with another member of staff or with the pastoral care staff that the pupil comes from a bad home and we build a mould for ourselves for the way in which we regard the child, the way we treat him and our expectations of him. It is very important for us to realise that a growing number of children are from homes where there are inherent difficulties and we need to give these pupils individual attention, rather than just giving them the faceless label of 'from a bad home'. If possible, we need to get to know the parents and the home situation of these young people in more detail than we would for other pupils. We need to make sure that the support and help we offer the child is in accordance with his actual circumstances and not just the circumstances we imagine him to be facing.

It is quite surprising sometimes how a young person can adapt to long-term alcoholism in parents and is able to cope with his home situation, until someone points out to him that he is different from other people because he has one or more parents who are experiencing problems with alcohol. Someone involving himself in the situation of a young person may therefore cause the person problems, but at the same time this should lead us to minimise the fact that many young people in such a situation are longing to be able to share their problems with someone. The sensitive teacher–counsellor must be able to tell the difference between the two stances, and be able to offer the right sort of help to the young person.

Experimenting with illicit drugs

Having considered in Chapter Six the *management* of situations where illicit drugs feature, we will now look at how the counsellor helps the young person who is experimenting. It is more likely that young people coming for help to the counsellor will be at the experimenting stage, rather than being addicted to drugs. Addiction counselling is very different from the counselling described in this section. When counselling young people who are experimenting, the first thing to find out from discussion with them, is what stage they have reached in drug-taking. Some of these stages are set out on p. 92 showing how drug-taking develops due to decisions being made.

Naturally other factors will affect such decisions but 'career lines' can be traced through which people develop their drug-taking.

A considerable amount of time has been wasted discussing with young people the progression from one drug to another. One can still, for instance, come across people who think that the natural progression from cannabis is to heroin. It is probably far more important to help young people see where they have come from, where they are going to and, most important of all, which stage they have reached at the present in relation to the drug they are using. The diagram above can be used in connection with any type of drug-taking, including alcohol and tobacco. The important fact is that one decision about behaviour predisposes the next decision. A young person would not have reached the third stage, for example, without having gone through the first two stages. The counsellor can help his client realise the decision he took to come to his present stage and the decisions he

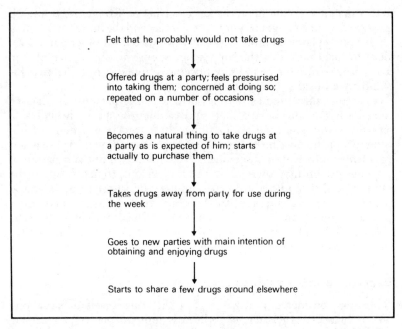

Felt that he probably would not take drugs

Offered drugs at a party; feels pressurised
into taking them; concerned at doing so;
repeated on a number of occasions

Becomes a natural thing to take drugs at
a party as is expected of him; starts
actually to purchase them

Takes drugs away from party for use during
the week

Goes to new parties with main intention of
obtaining and enjoying drugs

Starts to share a few drugs around elsewhere

will be forced to take in the future. This process is useful because
decisions can also be changed to effect a reversal of behaviour and
this can be discussed with the young person. As long as the pupil is
at the experimenting or heavy abuse stage, the counsellor with
experience should be able to deal with this problem as well as any
other problem of adolescents. This idea of decisions pre-empting
further decisions helps us to recognise that a 'drug problem' may be
about drugs of some type or another. However, it also can equally
or more likely be about other forms of behaviour, interpersonal
relationships, etc., when the drugs are a symptom of other factors.
When the young person is dependent (taking drugs *regularly* to
alleviate mental or physical pain or the effects of the previous dose),
however, there is then a case for the early introduction to an
outside agency.

The second piece of information the counsellor needs to discover is
what drug the young person is taking. Too many adults have looked
up the slang terms for drugs and tried to talk to young people in these
terms. There is really no need: most young people are perceptive
enough to realise that the adult does not mix in circles where these
terms are used, and that an adult using them is 'putting it on'.
Normally the young person will be able to state what drug he is
taking and the effects it has on him. Drugs used by early experimen-
ters tend to fall within one of the following groups.

(1) *Those that slow down the nervous system—barbiturates.* These are drugs which are often given for sleep. They are taken by young people to give a pleasant feeling of dreaminess and being at ease. There are also various depressant drugs which can act like barbiturates, but which are not strictly speaking in that class. Most of these have similar effects of depressant action like barbiturates. If taken in too great a quantity, or if taken in conjunction with another drug such as alcohol they can easily cause an overdose, unconsciousness or death. Tranquillisers, on the other hand, are taken mostly on prescription and are rarely sold illegally, because they are easily available legally. They have the same effect of taking the edge off situations, calming people down and making them feel more at ease. Large numbers of tranquillisers are, of course, prescribed each year in this country. Both of these groups of drugs can cause dependence. When such drugs are brought from an illegal source, it is unlikely that the person encouraging use will know the precise strength of each tablet—so there is no control over the variation in potency. Just because each tablet looks the same, it does not mean that they will have the same effect.

(2) *Those that stimulate the nervous system—amphetamines.* These are normally taken in tablet form. In some situations, a small amount may be injected. Amphetamines speed up the nervous system and make a person more talkative and more willing to laugh. They also keep people awake. Young people may therefore take them for either reason, to stay awake or to achieve a more prominent position in their social group. When the drug wears off, there is a rebound effect with feelings of depression and exhaustion, so that there is the temptation to take another, and so on, leading to deterioration and possible nervous collapse, also increase in irritability, aggression and intolerance. In the long term, even if taken only at weekends, amphetamines can create psychological dependence.

(3) *Cannabis/'pot'/'hash'.* This is a widely debated drug and as yet we do not fully know the effects of the different chemicals found in it. It is further complicated by the fact that samples of cannabis differ in the amount of chemicals present. Cannabis can be smoked, chewed and, very occasionally, sniffed. To some degree it basically acts as a depressant, having a slowing down effect, and to some extent as a hallucinogen, slightly altering one's way of perceiving things. Cannabis affects driving skills considerably, according to research which has been carried out. There are black marks against it in various pieces of research relating to physical or psychological problems in some individuals who use the drug. None of this research is conclusive and this is a considerable drawback when discussing cannabis with young people.

(4) *Hallucinogens, e.g. LSD (Lysergic acid) and STP (a similar substance).*

There are many substances which come into this catergory, usually manufactured illegally. They give what is called 'a trip'. This is an experience which can last for a considerable period of time, even up to twelve hours, where the person's sensory perception is totally muddled. The substance does not add anything to a person, but rather changes round the way that senses receive information and channel the information to the brain. LSD is one of the most potent drugs known to man and because it is sold in tablet form as microdots, which are made in various illegal drug factories, it is virtually impossible to gauge the exact strength of each tablet. Because the psychological effect that LSD induces is such an unusual one, there is always the risk of various psychotic states developing from its use. Also, because LSD distorts the perception of space and distance, there is an increased likelihood of accidents occurring under its influence.

(5) *There are a number of substances which look like a drug but are not.* Young people may be sold anything posing as a drug, but find that there is no psycho-active chemical in the substance. It has been known for camel dung to be sold as cannabis and for 'Smarties' and other sweets to be offered as barbiturates and amphetamines. The problem this can cause is that if a person works out that what he has taken has produced no effect on him, or if he works out an imagined effect, the next time he may take a larger amount of something which may be a real chemical and may cause an overdose.

Many young people quite quickly start using several drugs simultaneously. At some stage it is worth discussing with them the interaction of drugs and particularly the interaction of drugs with alcohol.

The third point for the counsellor to discover is why his client started taking drugs. This information is important because it can help the counsellor to decide on the course he should take in his counselling. There are a wide variety of reasons why young people start to take drugs, but the reasons can be summarised into three main ones as follows.

Starting on drugs

(1) *Situational*
The young person finds himself in a setting where he feels forced to act in a certain way. In the context of drug-taking, the person therefore feels he has to take drugs.

Faced with a young person in this situation, the counsellor needs to look at all the possible alternatives. An experienced counsellor will know better than to say: 'This is the correct one to follow', for nobody, however sensitive, can fully appreciate the situational pressures upon another person. For example, the counsellor needs to discuss whether the client could go round with another group; could he go with a friend, so that they could both leave together at some stage? Is it possible for the young person to say he does not like the drug, having tried it, and decline? All these sorts of issues need to be talked through. Progress is made by looking once more at the decision-making process to see what the next stage before the client is likely to be. A good deal has been said about exploring situations with young people. Of course, this can mean anything from 'Tell me what happened', to a full analysis of the ways in which a young person could cope with the situation. Seldom do we make full use of the circumstances which people actually face for doing work with them to help them to cope better.

Below are suggested a number of areas which are related to real life situations and which can be explored with young people. The way a person responds to a situation will be determined by a range of elements which will affect him in differing degrees.

(a) *Information and knowledge.* If someone is riding a motorbike and he leaves a party after smoking 'pot', his knowledge about the effect of cannabis on driving skills may have some effect on the way he responds to cannabis-smoking.

(b) *Previous experience.* If a person finds that he suffers by taking a certain course of action, such as smoking cannabis for too long, another time he may not do so. On the other hand, he may have found the experience pleasurable and do it again with a vengeance!

(c) *Values.* These are the general, global concepts a person may have concerning behaviour. They will include values such as risk-taking, health, independence, responsibility, values about the law.

(d) *Attitudes.* These are much more specific views about defined subjects. One may, for instance, have an attitude for or against smoking, or the attitude that smokers' health deteriorates, or the attitude of respect or otherwise for the non-smoker.

(e) *Situational constraints.* These are probably the most important influences. They include the expected behaviour in a setting (taking turns to smoke cannabis in a round at a party), peer group pressures (which can force people to behave in a certain way), opinion leaders (the person who others follow, who is not necessarily the loudest person), significant other people (the likely reaction of those important to the person such as parents and girlfriend/boyfriend).

The results of all these elements will be that, when a young person finds himself in a drug situation, the most important element to him will be the situational constraints. Recent research suggests that this element will then modify his attitudes and predict his future attitudes to such situations. In other words, if he takes 'pot' with a group of people who commonly do so, then his previous attitude that taking 'pot' was dangerous will probably change.

(2) *Experimental*

The young person likes the experience he gets from taking drugs. The first question we always ask people who refer those who are drug-takers for counselling is, 'Do they want to stop?' The answer is very often, 'Of course not, but I think they should!' If a person takes drugs because he enjoys them with no reservations, it is unlikely that counselling will stop him doing so. Depending on a school's attitude, it may be feasible for the counsellor to aim rather at lowering the consequences of drug-taking. In a group taking cannabis as part of its cultural heritage, for example, the counsellor could discuss with them the possible problems caused by long term use and the effect on skills such as driving. This approach would obviously not be acceptable in all schools and the approach to be taken would have to be decided through the staff discussions on how best to cope with incidents.

Young people taking drugs often enjoy the effects of the drug, but are still also concerned to some degree. The issues which may be discussed with these fall into two groups: in the first group the problems are associated with whether the young person has a satisfactory control over the drug's constituents or dosage. With a drug known as 'blues', the constituents could be any of a number of drugs. The strength of any illicit drug can vary from one day's supply to another. Discussion with the person must cover whether he is prepared to take that sort of risk, bearing in mind that adolescence is the time for taking risks.

The second group of issues occurs in the exceptional circumstances when the counsellor is faced with a crisis, such as a young person telephoning him when on a bad LSD trip. Here the counsellor will need to assess how bad the situation is and, if possible, go to the person. If physical complications seem to be present, i.e. if he has harmed himself or possibly taken something else as well and breathing is affected, then there will be a case for hospital treatment. Very often, however, a friend can 'talk him down', by encouraging him to talk about what he was doing before the trip and what he will do after it, so that the young person will realise that these effects are temporary and by moving him into an environment with neutral stimuli so that he can be calmed down. A trip can last for up to twelve hours, so the counsellor will have to be patient! Sometimes the early user of cannabis can experience a similar bad reaction and will need the same support and comfort. In these circumstances, the way for further counselling is made obvious.

Naturally this type of counselling is unlikely to be the lot of the classroom teacher, but it will apply to those counsellors and youth workers who do counselling work out of school.

(3) *Underlying problems*
There used to be a tendency for psychiatrists to suggest that all addicts would have needed treatment, even if they had never taken drugs. This is not true. Obviously a person with a mental condition will reach a serious stage of drug-taking more quickly, but most psychiatrists tend only to see people suffering from the effects of drug-taking over a long period of time. Many normal young people, however, have serious problems at some stages in their lives. The problems become out of perspective and drugs introduced at this stage may seem to sort out or block out the problems. In cases like these, the counsellor would be wise to leave the drug aspect for the time being and look instead at the underlying causes. As the person is helped to sort out some of the problems, see that others could also be resolved and come to terms with those problems that will always exist, then the counsellor can help his client to reconsider whether his drug-taking is really necessary. If a young person is leaving school, the good counsellor will ensure that his client knows he can still come back to chat and gain support. The counsellor will also try to help the person find others away from the school context to whom he can relate and from whom he can receive support.

Glue-sniffing

Every so often a different area gets an outbreak of glue-sniffing. The reactions range from totally ignoring it to bringing in the Drugs Squad, neither of which reactions are likely to be useful in this particular context.

In an attempt to discourage young people from glue-sniffing, glue has been attributed with all sorts of possible harmful effects and one would almost expect multiple illnesses to occur as a result of using glue in the woodwork lesson, if some of the more sensational writings on the subject were to be believed. To summarise the present position, we can say the following: glues contain chemicals and these chemicals are said to have harmful effects on various organs of the body if taken in large quantities; the results of research into the subject are inconclusive and one would suspect that the amount it is possible to sniff is unlikely, in fact, to affect these organs.

Having said this, the main cause for concern is the arresting of breathing. The vapours from glue, if taken into the bloodstream, can displace oxygen and therefore cause muzzy headaches which the users seek. In so doing it is possible to supply so little oxygen to the brain that unconsciousness or death may occur. Glues are very unpredictable in their effects. A sniffer cannot measure the amount he is taking in and unsciounesss may occur without the person recognising any early signs. Young people take risks as a normal part of adolescence. To lay too much emphasis on the risks of taking chemicals may merely encourage them to take even more for even greater risk. As human beings develop, they learn acceptable risk-taking procedures and put more constraints upon when they are prepared to take risks. It may be that instead of concentrating upon the risks of glue-sniffing, we would do better to stress that it is an uncontrolled risk, i.e. not an acceptable one, for the user cannot know how much he is taking and therefore cannot know when to stop at a certain stage.

In the handling of any incident of glue-sniffing, other aspects need to be borne in mind. Firstly, it is not illegal. The police cannot do anything if glue is bought, except perhaps make it seem even more of a risk to the young people who buy it. There is no age at which people cannot use it and there is little parents can do to forbid its use or even find out if it is being used. From the other extreme of this lack of knowledge, if anyone makes excessive fuss about glue-sniffing the Press will quickly claim that there is now an 'incident' in their area and tell young people which glues to use.

When a school finds out that glue-sniffing occurs, there is no more important advice than to play the incident as quietly as possible. Once young people understand that it can cause arresting of breathing and once parents know what is going on, the incident cannot be the sole responsibility of the school. There is nothing legally which the school must do to deal with the incident, but there are some areas of support which can be carried out. Sniffing, for example, normally takes place in groups, so there may be members of the group who have doubts about what they are doing and need the support and counsel of someone outside the group. Secondly, as with other drugs, the reasons for using glue need to be looked at. If a young person uses glue out of curiosity, explaining its effect on breathing may help him to clarify his behaviour. If he uses it because of group pressure, this can be discussed. If he uses it because he likes the experience, the reason why he needs such an experience can be looked at sensitively. A pupil may possibly sniff glue in order to shock the school, a sign of rebellion, and in this case the school's response may be all important. Rather than over-reacting, the teacher needs to carefully determine the pupil's reason for using glue.

Over-the-counter drugs

There are various reasons why someone may start to take large quantities of over-the-counter drugs and the main reasons are discussed below.

One reason may be that the young person is copying one of his parents. This needs to be openly discussed by the counsellor and the young person so that the pupil can be helped to realise that these drugs are not necessarily safe unless they are used carefully.

A second reason could be that the person is suffering some pain, but is denying the fact. The drug he takes will presumably be a pain-killer. In such a case the counsellor needs to discover if the young person understands that a pain-killer will not cure the pain and if he has a reason for not going to the doctor—perhaps a date he does not want to miss—or if he is too scared to find out what is really wrong with him.

The third reason, sadly becoming more common these days, is that the person is slowly poisoning himself by taking anything and everything because he feels unwell. The more chemicals he takes, of course, the more unwell he feels. The counsellor needs to be alert to the early stages of such behaviour, and to explain to the young person the delicate chemical balance of the human body and the problems which will arise from trying to fill the body with all sorts of chemicals.

The fourth reason is also being seen more often today, when a young person who is attempting to become a drug-taker, cannot get hold of illicit drugs and so takes any drug he can find. Such a person might well believe that he is addicted to certain substances, but the counsellor should not necessarily believe this and must form his own judgement. Does the counsellor tell the young person that he is mistaken? One course of action, as stated before, is to explore behind the front of drug-taking to find the reasons for this behaviour.

With cases of people taking over-the-counter drugs, as in many different problems found in adolescence, the counsellor will need to do a considerable amount of work in helping young people develop coping skills.

Smoking

The counsellor firstly needs to discover through discussion with the pupil what sort of smoker he is and the strategies, as below, can then be discussed. The support and understanding of the counsellor can be helpful on its own.

Categories of smoker and strategies for those who want to give up are as follows.

(1) *The handling smoker* feels the need to handle something in order to alleviate tension when in a group. Alternatives to be discussed are chewing gum, twiddling a pencil, or even different ways of sitting.

(2) *The stimulation smoker* needs a cigarette to raise the energy to face the day. The trigger points need to be analysed, so that something could be put in its place, e.g. having a cup of coffee before the desire to smoke gets too great.

(3) *The group smoker* is triggered by others lighting up cigarettes or cigarettes being offered. This is perhaps one of the hardest groups to help. He should be helped to recognise the trigger so that he can at least watch for it.

(4) *The nicotine addict* who tends to breathe in a lot of smoke. This person has a physical addiction to nicotine. He needs to be made to recognise the fact and make a complete break.

Strategies for those who wish to cut down on cigarettes can include:
(1) starting to leave the last third of a cigarette;
(2) choosing a lower tar brand of cigarettes;
(3) smoking fewer cigarettes by noticing the signals which can cause them to light up;
(4) breathing the smoke out rather than inhaling.

It may be worthwhile for schools which have a group of young people who want to give up smoking to organise some sort of group to help them. It is often a good idea for staff member who wants to give up smoking to join the group, in order to demonstrate that it is not just a matter of school rules, but a group of people genuinely wanting to give up smoking. In these groups, various things can be done, e.g. graphs can be drawn to see how long various people have been able to stay off cigarettes and how many people have cut down, and encouragement can be given within the group. With a more sophisticated or older group, there can be discussion between the various members about the different situations which they find difficult and which push them back into smoking. Suggestions can be given as to how to cope with these pressures.

Some areas run smoking withdrawal clinics, although these tend to attract a slightly older age range than school pupils, but if a young person is on his own in the school with this problem, a referral to a smoking withdrawal clinic may help him. The teacher must make sure that he does not give simplistic answers about ways of giving up. It may well be worthwhile to involve teachers who have at some time given up smoking and have had to face the difficulty of going without a cigarette. Constant encouragement is necessary for the person trying to give up and if a person manages to give up or cut down for a short period, but then goes back to smoking heavily, one should not write the person off at this stage. He may well want to try to give up again at another stage and will again need the support and encouragement, though perhaps of a different kind.

The majority of smokers find it easier to give up abruptly rather than gradually cutting down on cigarettes. One study of ex-smokers' methods of giving up showed that 96 per cent gave up abruptly and 4 per cent gradually; 12 per cent used 'medicine aids' to help them give up; 58 per cent gave up of their own accord, and 21 per cent gave up on the basis of doctors' advice.

Various smoking withdrawal aids are available. Chemical aids, such as substances in a chewing gum, mouthwash or aerosol, may act unpleasantly as aversion therapy when they react with tobacco smoke. There are mechanical aids, such as dummy cigarettes and various forms of filters, and herbal cigarettes and various placebo tablets and capsules may be helpful.

8

In conclusion

The good teacher-counsellor must beware of gaining an entourage of those who are dependent. There is a possibility that those who counsel feel so committed to an individual who is troubled that they become a father-confessor for too much of the young person's life. In relation to drugs, a young person with a dependent personality may well exchange the counsellor for the drug, if the counsellor is too directive and supportive. Obversely, the counsellor who is totally non-directive may well find with some people that nothing changes, as some types of drugs bring about the inability to think clearly, to take decisions and discover motivations. A balance is clearly needed. It is a paternal instinct to keep a troubled person close for support, but sometimes it may be better if links are reduced and the person taught to be independent. The counsellor must therefore have the strength to know when to break a relationship with an individual or group. The paternal counsellor, happy to hand out advice on everything to dependent young people, is hastening the dawn of Orwell's 1984.

Truax and Carkhuff* argue that poor counselling can be a potentially sinister development and can become a device for restoring a teacher despotism. We have a strong belief in the sincerity and sensitivity of the majority of teachers and we deplore the cynical criticism of much caring pastoral work done in schools. Caring is a normal school activity, not a professional specialism. Yet having said that, we have to agree with counselling colleagues who point to poor schools and careless colleges, where a cynicism of welfare and counselling activities reduces the humanity of the staff and where instruction seems to supersede education. An ill-led institution's counselling may be only a device to reinforce the authority of the school and to provide a window dressing. The outsider who is aware of student problems can see this misuse of counselling, but institutional hierarchies can be powerful in resisting change, and the true image of counselling is devalued.

* Truax, C. and Carkhuff, R. *Towards effective counselling and psychotherapy* Aldine, Chicago, 1967.

Such warnings about bad or inneffectual counselling and pastoral care must be heeded: counselling can merely divert attention from the work of inadequate institutions, can be intrusive when clumsily done and can be a coercive device of authority. Knowing that there can be misuse of counselling must not however, devalue well-planned counselling schemes which have a sense of humility. A sensitive team approach is likely to avoid dangers. We must offer a repertoire of counselling to all pupils and students and it is likely that this will be at two levels: the level of the teacher-counsellor who has some extra skill and time, supporting other colleagues who are often the first contact with young people; and, alternatively, through referral, deeper counselling dealt with by more expert people. A critical point is whether there is an understanding by teacher-counsellors and class tutors of their limitations plus an awareness in observing those who should be referred elsewhere, and a responsible developmental approach to counselling as a team responsibility.

There is a temptation for people who are concerned with the mechanics of living and teaching in an institution to forget that all they do is based on good relationships. The fact that young people are reasonably ordered and apparently spend their time listening in large groups, sometimes overlays the basic fact that learning does not take place unless there is motivation and unless people feel valued and significant. Since a great deal of what is happening in society is reducing the significance of individuals, a struggle to affect this must be reflected in schools and colleges. There is a growing mood of questioning and yet a dangerous level of apathy. The two seem to be opposites, yet both are increasing; the questioning is tending, because of a lack of positive leadership and direction, towards aggression; the apathy is shown in rejection of authority and an abandonment of thinking to pressure groups. Society seems to be offering a polarisation between productivity and personal happiness. We are teaching people to have more expectations of life but we are not necessarily teaching them how to achieve these. Many teachers are questioning the purpose of education and are questioning the traditional type of academic qualifications. Is education solely to do with qualifications and efficiency? Is it not also to do with personal happiness and the needs of individuals and with learning to live? So, counselling and pastoral care are to do with efficient learning, but are also linked in purpose with a more caring society.

If we consider the demands of a competitive economy, particularly the need for qualifications, and if we see how schools and colleges are increasingly devoted to this demand for academic and technical competence, it is equally easy to see that the more personal side of living can be regarded as only of marginal significance—as a first-aid system offered as a sweetener to busy institutions. This misses the whole point of education in personal relationships and misses the whole point of the counselling element of the work. We are not only concerned with a first-aid system of crisis counselling of a paternal kind, we are much more concerned with a positive element of education which can be more than just a side-track and could conceivably be the way we demonstrate better values in society. If apathy and aggression continue to develop, then not only will the quality of our living be questionable, but the total social cost of dealing with apathetic and aggressive groups can be immense. Surely there must be ways in our schools and colleges for diversion of these social ills.

To refer now to our concern for better health education, we must argue forcibly for better planning in this area of the curriculum. If, for example, we look at the effects of smoking and abuse of alcohol in society, we have sad evidence both in purely financial and in human terms. Studies have pointed to the fact that the costs of abuse outweigh the tax revenue in, for instance, a country's use of tobacco. It seems logical to believe that schools and colleges have an important role in helping young people to come to terms with the fact that chemicals are widely used and that harm from them can be radically reduced. This will pay dividends in human and economic terms and in helping young people to cope well with their social environments and to be orientated towards learning.

The 'counselling' of individuals and groups is at the heart of pastoral care. It is an omnibus word and applies to all people throughout their lives. It includes befriending, as well as more professional therapy. It applies to individuals and to groups; it is people helping people to understand a complicated environment and it is people caring for people as a demonstration of what being human is about.

'All the world is queer except thee and me, and even thee, I suspect, is a little queer', said a Quaker. Problems are part of a normal life, and so should be good counselling.

Appendix A

Selected books and curriculum materials

Pastoral care, counselling and group work

Argyle, M., *The Psychology of Inter-personal behaviour*, Pelican 1972.

Bolger, A. W., *Child Study and Guidance in Schools*. Constable, 1975.

Blackburn, K., *The Tutor*, Heinemann Educational, 1975.

Blackham, H. (Ed.). *Ethical Standards in Counselling*, Bedford Square Press, 1974.

Button, L., *Development Group Work with Adolescents*, ULP, 1974.

Cauthery, P., *Student Health*, Priory Press, 1973.

Gallagher, J. R. and Harris, H. I., *Emotional Problems of Adolescents*, OUP, 1976.

Haigh, G., *Pastoral Care*, Pitman Publishing, 1975.

Haigh, G., *The Reluctant Adolescent*, Temple Smith, 1976.

Hamblin, D. *The Teacher and Counselling*, Blackwell, 1974.

Hamblin, D. *The Teacher and Pastoral Care*, Blackwell, 1978.

Hargreaves, D., *Inter-personal Relations and Education*, Routledge and Kegan Paul, 1975.

Holden, A., *Counselling in Secondary Schools*, Constable, 1971.

Hughes, P. M., *Guidance and Counselling in Schools*, Pergamon Education, 1971.

Irwin, E. M., *Growing Pains*, Macdonald and Evans, 1977.

Jones, A., *Counselling Adolescents in Schools*, R.K.P., 1977.

Lancs, C. C., *Pastoral Care and EPR in Lancashire Secondary Schools*, Lancashire Education Committee, 1978.

Lancs, C. C., *Student Counselling in Lancashire*, Lancashire Education Committee, 1979.

Laufer, M. *Adolescent Disturbance and Breakdown*, MIND and Penguin, 1975.

Lobo, E. de H., *Children of Immigrants to Britain, their Health and Social Problems*, Hodder and Stoughton, 1978.

Lytten, H. and Craft, M., *Guidance and Counselling in British Schools*, Arnold, 1974.

Marland, M., *Pastoral Care*, Heinemann Educational, 1974.

Newsome, Thorn and Wyld, *Student Counselling in Practice*, ULP, 1973.

Rogers, C. R., *Client-Centred Therapy*, Houghton-Mifflin (USA), Constable, 1965.

Rowe, A., *The School as a Guidance Community*, Pearson, 1971.

Sim, M. *Tutors and the Students*, Livingstone, 1970.

Taylor, H. J. F., *School Counselling,* Macmillan, 1971.
Wolff, S., *Children under Stress,* Pelican, 1973.

Health education, drugs, alcohol and tobacco

Caruana, S., Cowley, J. C. P. and Rutherford, D., *Teaching about Alcohol and Drinking,* TACADE, 1978.
Dalzell Ward, A *Textbook of Health Education,* Tavistock, 1974.
DES, *Drugs and the Schools,* DES, 1972.
DES, *Health Education in Schools,* HMSO, 1977.
DES, *Health Education in Secondary Schools,* Evans/Methuen Educational, 1976.
DES, *Smoking and Health in Schools,* DES, 1972.
Dorn, N., *Teaching Decision-making Skills about Legal and Illegal Drugs,* HEC/ISDD, 1977.
Hawker, A., *Adolescents and Alcohol,* Edsalls, 1978.
Irwin, V. and Spira, M., *Basic Health Education,* Longman, 1977.
Kessel, N. and Walton, H., *Alcoholism,* Pelican, 1969.
Lea, M. V., *Health and Social Education,* Heinemann Educational, 1975.
Parish, P., *Medicines: A Guide for Everybody,* Penguin, 1976.
Parker, E. W., *An Introduction to Health Education,* Macmillan Educational, 1975.
Schools Council, *Working Paper 57: Health and Education in Secondary Schools,* Evans/Methuen Educational, 1976.
TACADE, *Alcohol Basic Facts,* TACADE, 1977.
TACADE, *Drugs Basic Facts,* TACADE, 1976.
TACADE, *Guidelines for Parents,* TACADE, 1976
TACADE, *Smoking Fact Sheets,* TACADE, 1977.
Willis, M. and McLachlan, M. E., *Medical Care in Schools,* Edward Arnold, 1977.
Zacune, J. and Hessman, C. *Drugs, Alcohol and Tobacco in Britain,* Heinemann, 1971.

Selected curriculum materials for use in health education and tutorial programmes

(1) *'Good Health' (Collins Educational)*

An integrated course for 9–13 years.
1. Our Bodies
2. Our Safety
3. Our Families
4. Our Lives

The quality of life as its relates to the health of the individual, his family, the community and the environment is the keynote of the project. Each unit comprises ten copies of the work book, twenty-eight different cards and a teacher's guide.

(2) *'Situations' (Blackie)*

Situations 1 (Fourth-year pack)
Situations 2 (Fifth-year pack)
English material based almost entirely on social situations. Developed by the serving teachers of the North-West Curriculum Development Project. Intended for Fourth- and Fifth-year students. The 'situations' of the title are not topics, but open-ended teaching units. Pupils are encouraged to interpret accurately a scene, emotion, or event, presented by literature, slides, photographs, taped songs, sound or speech, and to compare it with their own experience. The early situations concern mainly adolescents; the fifth-year course moves towards a more objective study of adult relationships.

(3) *The Childwall Project—'Design for Living' (E. J. Arnold & Son Ltd, 1972–74)*

This is a social studies course for children of average and below average ability structured to occupy half-a-day per week of their last two years in school. It is an integrated course in the sense that concepts and techniques of many disciplines are introduced when the pupils require them to explore a particular problem.

Each theme is subdivided into topics. Materials within the kit, often a tape recording, provide the 'impact' necessary to motivate the pupils to investigate the background to a topic. The next section of each topic, entitled 'enquiry', is where skills and concepts are acquired. Finally, the pupils re-assess the problem with the benefit of their newly-acquired knowledge.

Each theme is produced as a self-contained kit with material for the teacher and twenty pupils. Additional pupils' materials are available only in packs of ten.

(a) *Responsibilities of adulthood*
Covers the problems encountered in early adolescence. It looks at relationships with adults, and with other adolescents and at areas of conflict which occur at home and at school.
The theme is developed by study of the physical and emotional changes of adolescence. Finally, courtship and marriage are dealt with from both romantic and practical aspects.

(b) *Understanding Children*
Deals with the development and birth of babies, emotional and physical needs of children, relationships between children and parents, children and the law, family planning and the history of education.

(c) *The World of Work*
Deals with the choice of a job and its difficulties, writing letters of application, preparing for interviews, consideration of job prospects and training programmes, relationships at work, trade unions, the Common Market, the organisation of industry, unemployment and leisure.

(d) *Living Today*
Deals with the social problems and issues relating to the community. These include neighbourliness, vandalism, moving to a new estate, the town hall, the mentally handicapped, social change and growing old.

(e) *The World Around Us*
Deals with our political responsibilities and with issues of national interest.

These include elections, Parliament, the national economy, politics abroad, pollution, conservation, nationalism, immigration and emigration, war, ideologies and development of other countries.

(4) Breakaway Series (Hulton Educational Publications Ltd, 1973–77)

Of special interest:
Book 1—*People with Problems*
Book 2—*Finding a job and settling down*
Book 5—*Keeping the peace*
Fifteen books in the series and thirty topics in each book, each of which is given double-page treatment. On the left, a strip cartoon treatment of topics such as 'Boredom', 'The Drug Addict', 'The Unmarried Mother', 'The Lonely Teenager', 'Under stress'; with further reading and 'Things to Do' on the right-hand page.

(5) Connexions (Penguin)

Seventeen titles which include:
Break for Commercials
Disaster
Fit to Live in
For Better, for Worse
His and Hers
The Language of Prejudice
Shelter
Violence
Work
Magazine-style topic books suitable for non-academic pupils.

(6) The Schools Council/Nuffield Humanities Curriculum Project (Heineman Educational Books Ltd, 1971)

'The Family'
'Relations between the sexes'
'Poverty'
'People and Work'
'Law and Order'
'Living in Cities'
'Education'
'War and Society'
   (For pupils aged 14–16)
   The method of using this project is as important as the material, which is not aimed at lower ability pupils.
   For each topic the material is available in the following forms.
   Complete pack, comprising:
(a) Students' element—about 200 items of 'evidence'—poems, plays, extracts

from newspapers, photographs etc. Each item is packed in sets of twenty in a separate polythene bag and colour coded for easy storage.
(b) Teachers' element—two sets of each piece of evidence, each set packed in an indexed envelope: two general introductions to the project: two teachers' handbooks for that topic: a set of tapes with about three hours of recorded material (poems, plays, interviews, songs): film order forms. Teachers' element only—as (b) above.

(7) Thinkstrips (Longman)

Comics based on social and health topics to help teenagers to imagine the situations they will meet and the decisions they will have to make. Designed especially for less academic 14–16-year-olds, but suitable for all abilities. They provide points for discussion and suggestions for projects and activities including role play. Titles: 'It's your round', (drink); 'It'll never be the same, (parenthood); 'It's only fair, (personal relationships).

(8) You and Your Parents, You and Your Environment, (Macmillan Education)

These are two kits in the Viewfinder series; they aim to encourage pupils to see themselves in relation to their families and to the wider community to which they belong. The kits contain teacher's notes, pamphlets, case studies and 'view charts' on which pupils can record their opinions and reactions. They are designed to be used with pupils of average and below average ability and could well form a basis on which teachers and pupils could build their own collection of material.

(9) General Studies Project (Longman/Penguin)

Intended for 16–18-year-old post 'O' level students. Can be adapted for use with younger and less academic students. Annual subscription covers catalogue of 100 Study Units, and 350 vouchers for further copies of Units. Units are catalogued under eleven themes, including Environment, Family, Population, Science and Responsibility.

(10) Schools Council Project: Health Education 5–13 (Nelson & Sons, 1977)

This is based on a very wide interpretation of 'health', encompassing not only hygiene and physical health and development, but also many emotional, social and environmental facts of human life.
The project provides excellent and strongly recommended material in three parts:
1. 'All about Me' for ages 5–8, a teachers' guide.
2. 'Think Well' for ages 9–13, a set of eight teachers' guides.
3. Pupils' materials.

(11) *Schools Council Health Education Project 13–18*

This project, moving into a dissemination phase during 1980 based on Southampton University has produced aids for in-service education of teachers in health education in schools for the age group 13–18. It is also concerned with developing materials for this age group.

(12) *Health Education Council Project: 'Living Well'—Health Education 12–18 (Cambridge University Press, 1977)*

Directed by Peter McPhail, this provided excellent discussion and teaching material on personal relationships and health topics.

'How are we feeling today?' A pack of thirty illustrated cards intended to stimulate discussion on topics related to health and relationships. Questions and suggestions for further work are printed on the reverse; full teacher's notes are included.

'Support Group'. A pack of thirty illustrated cards, centring on the theme of support for individuals with a variety of personal difficulties. A few cards requiring immediate solutions (e.g. First Aid) are included. Questions and suggestions for further work are printed on the reverse; full teacher's notes are included.

'Who Cares?' A set of thirty relationship studies in which young people are seen interacting with a variety of adults—teachers, youth club leaders, counsellors, parents and work supervisors. This pack will be especially suitable for use with 16–18-year-old students. Teacher's notes included.

(13) *Professional Development Workshop Manual (Health Education Council 1979)*

This manual forms the basis of school based in-service education for schools catering for children in the age group 5–13. It concentrates upon health education, but raises questions which are central to curriculum review generally. It is available through regionally appointed trainers.

(14) *Alcohol objectives workshop (TACADE)*

This is a ready made course designed to help teachers to assess the needs of children *vis-à-vis* alcohol and to design an educational programme for different age groups.

(15) *Family Life/Child Development/Parenthood Education in Schools*

In-service education of teachers section, The Open University. This project is producing a wide range of pupil and in-service aids related to the above themes and overlapping with health education. Published materials should become available from early 1981 although schools can be involved in a variety of ways before that date.

The In-Service education of teachers section is planning to increase its contribution to health, social and personal education in schools.

(16) *Open to Question (Richard Nicholson, Edward Arnold)*

A series of discussion starting points for pupils aged 14–18. The approach is open-ended and the material is in the form of newspaper articles, interviews, advertisements and photographs.

(17) *Dilemmas (David Walker, Edward Arnold)*

Short plays on moral and social problems.

(18) *Mind Out (Jane Moran, Edward Arnold)*

Plays and pages of facts on problems of alcohol, smoking, gambling, drugs, crime and sex.

(19) *Problem Page (Sue Porter, Edward Arnold)*

Resource material in areas of ethics and human relationships, covering problems at school, at homes and with the opposite sex.

(20) *Checkpoints (General Editor: John Foster, Edward Arnold)*

Very useful booklets on many topics, for average and below average pupils aged 14–16. Information, discussion points, writing and project work are included.

(21) *The Root of the Matter (H.R.H. Davies, Edward Arnold)*

Thirty topics for fourth- and fifth-year pupils on a wide range of problems relevant to the world today.

(22) *Enquiries (W. J. Hanson, Longman)*

A useful series of books for students aged 14–17 on fundamental social topics.

Appendix B

Useful agencies

Action on Smoking and Health,
Margaret Pyke House,
27/35 Mortimer Street,
London W1A 4QW,
Tel: 01-637-9843

National Institute for Careers
Education and Counselling,
Bateman Street,
Cambridge CB2 1LZ,
Tel: 0223-51446

British Association for Counselling,
26 Bedford Square,
London WC1 3HU

Health Education Council,
78 New Oxford Street,
London WC1A 1AH,
Tel: 01-637-1881

In-Service Education of Teachers Section,
PECU, Open University,
P.O. Box 188
Milton Keynes,
Buckinghamshire

Institute for the Study of Drug Dependence,
Kingsbury House,
3 Blackburn Road,
London NW6 1XA,
Tel: 01-328-5541

Institute of Health Education,
14 High Elms Road,
Hale Barns,
Cheshire

Medical Council on Alcoholism,
3 Grosvenor Crescent,
London SW1X 7EL,
Tel: 01-235-4182

National Council on Alcoholism,
3 Grosvenor Crescent,
London SW1X 7EL,
Tel: 01-235-4182

National Marriage Guidance Council,
Little Church Street,
Rugby,
Warwickshire,
Tel: Rugby 73241

Scottish Health Education Unit,
21 Landsdowne Crescent,
Edinburgh EH12 5EH,
Tel: 031-337-3251

TACADE,
(Health Education Development Unit and
Teachers' Advisory Council on Alcohol and Drug Education),
2 Mount Street,
Manchester M2 5NG,
Tel: 061-834-7210

Your local Health Education team.

Appendix C

A report on student counselling

A report of a working party of Lancashire Further and Higher Education teachers

(1) *Introduction*

Colleges should be guidance committees, enabling students to gain qualifications and skills in a caring atmosphere which is widely educational as well as instructional.

(2) *The Principles of Counselling*

Counselling is concerned with creating opportunities and environments for the personal, social, educational and vocational growth of the individual. It is based on attitudes about the value and worth of human beings, as well as their right to determine their own fulfilment. But a counsellor is equally concerned with skills which allow for the development of meaningful counselling relationships, the growth of insight, the offering of a range of alternative approaches and the support of the student as he determines and copes with his needs or difficulties. Counselling is a learning process for both counsellor and student because of the dynamic quality of the encounter and relationship.

(3) (a) *The aims of counselling*

The role of the counsellor has been identified as the promotion of positive mental health.
It follows then that *student counselling:*
 (i) aims to contribute to continuous growth in the development of individuals;
 (ii) attempts to deal with problems at the stage before they become critical;
 (iii) is mostly concerned with 'normal' students under stress;
 (iv) must have therapeutic elements, but should not attempt an over-ambitious psychiatric approach;
 (v) ensures that deeply disturbed students can have access to qualified specialist help;
 (vi) deals with a wide range of work from providing simple information and

re-assurance, to identifying and referring to expert help, severe personality breakdowns and behavioural problems.
(b) *Preventive or developmental counselling,* through class and tutorial group discussion, aims to consider:
human needs;
the situations and problems of young adults;
problems of communication, including the difficulty of making meaningful personal relationships;
the development of the capacity to make decisions and accept responsibility, within and without a college community;
the development of effective study habits;
(c) *Personal counselling,* on a one-to-one basis, with tutors and counsellors aims;
to help the student to identify his needs and to make a more effective interpretation of a situation;
to help him develop coping strategies—many problems cannot be solved and in these cases the function of the counsellor is to help the student to accept the situation and design constructive ways of coping with it;
to help him become more self-directive.

(4) *A counselling service*

Counselling is for all students, and not just for the minority who appear to have serious problems. It follows that counselling on this scale must be undertaken by a team.
(a) *The first level of counselling* is for the main body of students: it is largely *preventive* in nature and is often best dealt with on a group basis, sometimes being termed *'group work counselling'*. It takes advantages of student participation, acknowledging that many students are influenced by the attitudes of their peers more than they are by the attitudes of adults. In group discussions students can be helped to draw on the wide range of experience that each brings to the group; this is an important part of counselling service and the part which is most frequently neglected. It is sometimes assumed that this work is informally dealt with by every concerned teacher, but there is seldom justification for this view; there needs to be a planned and positive approach for this work.
(b) Closely linked with this general approach to counselling through group work, is the personal *tutorial system*. All students in a college should be linked with a personal tutor who is responsible, either on an individual one-to-one basis or through tutorial group discussion, for knowing and supporting the student in his college work and personal development. Tutors and class teachers, of course, can often detect early signs of stress and can either help the student to find the answer to problems or can ensure proper referral of a problem. This is fundamental level of counselling in a college.
(c) There is another level. There have been a number of surveys attempting to determine the proportion of students who need extra help and it has been suggested that on average this amounts to some 10 per cent in any institution. (Note that these are not 'disturbed' students but 'normal' students who are under particular stress at that time.) Counselling for these students is

primarily on a one-to-one basis. Because of the numbers involved and because they are usually dealt with in *personal counselling* situations no single counsellor could cope and a team of part-time counsellors is advisable.

(d) Some colleges may be able to justify a *full-time counsellor*, with specialist professional training. The full-time counsellor is in no way a substitute for the system outlined above. He must have the role of co-ordinator; he is also a consultant for other members of staff who handle many of the students' problems themselves, but who are able to refer to him. He will inevitably do one-to-one counselling himself, for students who prefer to refer problems directly to him, and for students referred by other counselling colleagues.

(e) *Careers counselling:* this is an area in which specialist help is essential. Making careers decisions involves thinking about oneself, one's needs and values, as well as one's abilities and ambitions. It is, therefore, not possible to make a clear distinction between 'personal', 'academic/educational' or 'careers' counselling; indeed, it is whilst discussing their futures, that many students find that they are able to bring out and begin to work through their present problem. Whilst departmental vocational advice will often be important, it may be advisable to include in the college counselling team trained staff capable of assisting in this area, with access to the wide range of current information, and able to assist a student in his vocational exploration. Careers education should also be offered through the curriculum, and students should have access to systematic careers programmes that are responsive to individual needs.

(5) *The ethics of counselling*

(a) *The counsellor's approach.* There are many approaches to counselling. At the start of an interview counselling must be *exploratory* and the counsellor should not impose his own ideas or suggest solutions; rather, he helps the student to make a realistic assessment of his situation. Once the problem is identified, the student and counsellor may perceive possible solutions, though the student may not have the ability to implement them. At this stage, there can be a need for a *positive* approach, in which the counsellor plays an advisory, constructive role. Continuing support and encouragement may be needed to enable the student to cope with a situation and ultimately to become self-reliant.

(b) *Referral.* Counsellors may need to refer students to other staff, or to agencies and specialist help, for they will not be qualified to help in every counselling situation. Counsellors should:
  (i) have sufficient time to know contacts in a wide number of agencies (such as medical, psychiatric, and hospital services, social services, voluntary bodies, probation, police and legal aid) so that a working relationship is established;
  (ii) discuss with the student whether referral is needed, when it should be sought and be able to suggest varying agencies offering help;
  (iii) be prepared to make the referral with or for the student if necessary, continuing to offer support as required.

(c) *Confidentiality.* To balance the needs of the individual and the requirements of an institution must in the end be a matter for the personal conscience and the professional judgement of the counsellor. As the counsellor has no special protection in law, conflicts of judgement may be inevitable at times. Many counsellors point to the need to be detached from authority, and stress the confidentiality of their role, and the need for information and sources to be kept confidential, unless consent to disclose their contents to others is given by the student. In practice, most students will agree to others being involved if it seems essential.

In the final analysis a counsellor is very much left to his or her own discretion, paying attention to the welfare of the individual and general well-being of the college and he needs the support and trust of the college authorities and his colleagues.

(6) *Summary*

Counselling is for all students and takes many forms. It must be an effective part of any college community and should involve all staff. A team of counsellors will be required, however, and training and a sufficient allocation of time are necessary. Whatever system is adopted must have the good-will and acceptance of the college community and may well need to be a phased development.

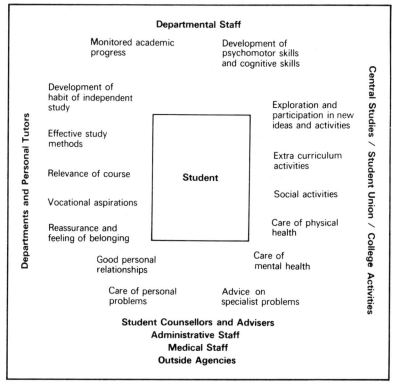

Appendix D

The law on drugs

Barbiturates: It is illegal to supply barbiturates without a prescription, but
not illegal to possess them. Some barbiturates are to be controlled when new legislation is introduced.

Tranquillisers: Normally prescribed.

Cannabis: Illegal to grow, supply or smoke cannabis or knowingly to allow premises to be used for the same without a licence for research from the Home Office. It is not an offence to possess without knowing.

LSD: Illegal to possess, manufacture or supply without a licence.

Amphetamine: Illegal to possess or supply without a prescription.

Tobacco: Cannot be sold to people under 16 years.

Alcohol: *Persons under 18:*
May not be supplied with alcohol in bars, or consume it in same.
May not purchase alcohol from off-licence premises.
May not be employed in bars during permitted hours.
May be employed in registered clubs.
Persons 16–18:
May be supplied with beer, porter, cider or perry on licensed premises with a meal, provided meal is not served in a bar.
Persons 14–16:
May be in a bar during permitted hours, but may not purchase, be supplied with or consume alcohol.
Persons under 14:
May not be in a bar of licensed premises during permitted hours, but (5–14 years) may legally be present in registered clubs.
Under 5
May not be given alcohol unless by medical order.

Appendix E

Drugs, alcohol and smoking: in-service training in schools

(1) It seems sensible that the school which is going to be able tactfully to handle even the most sensitive issues will be the one where the staff feel secure and united in a course of action. If a staff, or a working party of staff, discuss ways of handling incidents prior to their happening, there is a lot less chance of over-reaction.

The points raised below assume that there is a developed pastoral care system within a school.

(2) Smoking

(a) What rules exist concerning smoking in school; in the grounds; travelling to school? How realistic are these rules in relation to the smoking habits of the children? Do we know what the general habits are, or do we over/underestimate them by paying attention only to specific groups of children?
(b) Should there be different rules for different age groups?
(c) Are there different rules for different places? What about field trips? Holidays?
(d) Are there any points where conflict may arise between staff smoking habits and pupil smoking habits? Do any staff smoke when in the company of pupils? Are they allowed to?
(e) Is there pressure from any staff for a no-smoking area in the staff room?
(f) If a child breaks a school rule concerning smoking and is noticed by a teacher, what action should that teacher take? When does the teacher have to refer the child to others? To whom is the child referred?
(g) Is there any assistance for those wishing to give up smoking? Group sessions—perhaps of both staff and pupils?

(3) Prescribed/over-the-counter drugs

(a) Has the school any basic rules about bringing tablets and medicines into school?
(b) What procedures exist for those children who require daytime medication?
(c) What procedures exist for working out with parents the best way to administer doses of medicines needed regularly by some children?
(d) What procedure exists to inform the *relevant* staff when a child is under

medication which may affect his classroom behaviour or performance, (e.g. where a child is under the influence of tranquillisers).
(e) What procedure is adopted by the school on administering simple analgesics when requested by children?

(4) *Alcohol*

(a) What rules apply to consuming alcohol at school functions, before school functions, outside school functions (e.g. at dances and discos)?
(b) What should staff do if children re-enter a function having been drinking? Is there different action if they have been drinking from action taken only if they show signs of misbehaviour due to drinking?
(c) What should be the policy on the last day of term if a small group return having drunk alcohol at lunchtime? How can the minimum disturbance be achieved?
(d) Should teaching staff look at the consistency between their lunchtime drinking habits and that of some children?
(e) What aid can be given within the school if it becomes apparent that some children are drinking regularly?

(5) *Drugs used illicitly*

(a) In the school setting this is likely to be cannabis or pills (barbiturates or amphetamines). It is unlikely to take place in school and the main incidents coming to the notice of schools will be where a young person has been casually involved in one of his or her 'evening' peer groups.
(b) If a child reveals that they have been drawn into a situation where they have experimented with these drugs, what policy should the school adopt? Does the teacher have to inform the head teacher? Does he inform the pastoral head?
(c) If the information comes to the teacher from another source (e.g. other children), does this alter the policy resulting from previous paragraph's question?
(d) Should the police be informed?

(6) There exist a further series of questions which can be asked concerning the above themes.
(a) When should parents be notified in each instance? Is this to be done by a form teacher? A pastoral head? A head teacher?
(b) How can parents be involved in discussing the pastoral care of their children with staff?
(c) Are facilities available to refer children for specialist help if necessary? How comprehensive are these facilities? Do pastoral teachers meet with some of the social/health/support service workers in the catchment area?
(d) Are facilities available for pastoral staff to get advice to help them support individual children?
(e) What in-service training is available on pastoral care and counselling?

(7) Some children in the school may have parents or peers who have problems related to alcohol, drugs or tobacco. It is well accepted that a child with a parent who is suffering from alcoholism is likely to have many pressures on them which will affect their academic work. It seems reasonable that the school will have some role in helping the child, even if in a limited way.

Are there efficient lines of cojmunication between teachers and personnel in the area who work with families?

Is there a good understanding between teachers and such personnel of each other's strengths and weaknesses, and the constraints under which each profession works and the limitations of what can be done?

(8) Finally, the staff need to ask how many school rules on these themes need to be communicated to the pupils, bearing in mind that the more rules communicated, the more the staff are often tied as to the action they can take.

How can these methods of handling incidents be communicated to all staff, and also to new staff joining the school?

(9) Schools, like other places of employment, may have staff suffering from chemically-related problems. Industry is being urged to communicate to staff that they can go for treatment with their employment held open for them. The school community surely involves not only the children in it, but the staff. Can a school develop a system for supporting its staff over difficult periods?

Appendix F

An example of the advice to schools on drug education issued by Lancashire Local Education Authority

Drug education

(1) Drugs are misused by young people of school age of course, though usually away from school settings. Since we are a society which values and uses drugs very widely, misuse will probably continue and may increase among young people. Education about drugs, including alcohol and tobacco, is therefore an essential part of health education programmes in secondary schools.

(2) Courses are available in Lancashire to prepare selected teachers in drug education, and teachers attending such conferences and those attending pastoral work residential courses are given appropriate information and guidance on presentation.

Drug education conferences are organised periodically by the Lancashire Council on Alcohol and Drug Dependence and details are circulated to schools.

(3) It is obviously better to avoid over dramatising individual drug incidents. Drug education should not be highlighted and preferably should not be presented other than in a general pattern of health education or education in personal relationships. The problem should be presented as part of a balanced programme of tutorial guidance and counselling and as part of the interpretation of the social problems of society within schools. In this way, we should avoid the possibility of experimentation from excitement.

(4) Schools are advised to consider very carefully before using certain films for drug education as the subject can easily be wrongly emphasised. Visiting speakers may need to be reminded of our educational approach to drug education which is more concerned with 'Why?' than 'What?' and 'How?'. Increasing attention must be paid to education about alcohol and tobacco.

(5) The Education Authority has established an excellent liaison with the police on drug problems and we should look upon it as a duty to help them in any way we can in this connection. The police are more interested in the 'pusher' and the 'trafficker' than the young person experimenting with drugs. Whilst the police reserve the right to decide what action is right, they will certainly consider all the circumstances of an incident and what is best for the young person including seeking the advice of teachers before making their decision. The conviction of juveniles is not the main purpose of the police. If there are good relations between local police and the school staff, mutual trust

should develop. Regular meetings of social workers and police with school staff, especially those with pastoral responsibilities, are recommended to consider such social problems as drug misuse and under-age drinking.

(6) The Health Authority is very helpful with drug situations concerning individual pupils and with health education course planning; youth workers also are helpful in dealing with the problems of individual pupils.

(7) The Teachers' Advisory Council on Alcohol and Drug Education, 2 Mount Street, Manchester M2 5NG (061-834-7210), can be very helpful. Seminars for staffs of schools can be arranged. A periodic bulletin *Monitor* is published.

Appendix G

A checklist of themes for courses in schools and colleges

The following material provides a checklist of themes for courses in:
education for personal relationships;
family life education;
social and personal education;
moral and social education;
personal guidance;
health education.

This material can be the basis of:

(a) a regular timetabled series in all classes of a secondary school;
(b) regular tutorial work, co-ordinated with departmental teaching;
(c) short courses at appropriate times in each school year;
(d) co-ordinated work throughout all teaching departments, each accepting responsibility for certain topics or sections of topics at certain times;
(e) occasional residential experience courses;
(f) informal discussions in clubs or leisure settings.

The school setting

(a) Although it is clearly difficult to include such work as a separate series in an already full syllabus, many of the themes are essential in preparation for work and family life and are very relevant to the lives of pupils.
(b) Much of the work will already be included in departmental subject areas, but co-ordination and reinforcement are obviously essential.
(c) No attempt has been made to divide the subjects into school years and some topics are duplicated under different headings. It is desirable that many of the themes are dealt with each year from a different angle and in increasing depth.
(d) Head teachers may consider appointing a senior member of staff to co-ordinate the teaching of this work, and to guide other staff as to the best way of developing this teaching and discussion work. Certain aspects of the syllabus may be reinforced by help from colleagues in other services, especially in the Health Service.

The techniques employed include:

(a) gaining rapport with the group;
(b) spending some time on teaching but more on purposeful discussion;
(c) being prepared for questions of an unexpected nature;
(d) being conversant with the attitudes of the young and having some understanding of the language they use;
(e) the teacher expressing personal convictions positively and sincerely when they are sought and when they are appropriate.

The general aim

To help pupils to find information about human behaviour, to examine the values which people have found lead to personal happiness and stability in our society and to encourage pupils to develop standards in personal morality.

The objectives of the teacher

(a) To inform the adolescent about himself and his growing powers of mind and body.
(b) To help him form and develop stable relationships with others, accept other people and appreciate the value of tolerance.
(c) To help him face relationships with authority, with adults and with the other sex.
(d) To widen his horizons to the problems of humanity and to awaken an awareness of his responsibility towards his neighbours and community.
(e) To encourage him to explore and appreciate other people's beliefs, while developing his own.
(f) To help him to prepare for marriage and family life.
(g) To create a climate of opinion in schools that these themes are vitally important.
(h) Occasionally to act as counsellor for individuals, recognising those who require special treatment.

Themes

(1) Personal development

(a) The body and how it works—human biology.
(b) Reproduction and birth in the setting of family life and caring relationships.
(c) The growth and development of babies and children.
(d) Physical growth to maturity.
(e) Puberty—physical and psychological changes in adolescence.
(f) Emotional development.

(2) *The individual*

(a) Special advantages Man has over other animals.
(b) Learning processes and memory.
(c) Development of individual personalities.
(d) Moods and emotions.
(e) The influence of heredity and environment.
(f) Will-power and understanding ourselves.
(g) Self-control and co-operation as essential for civilised life.
(h) Conscience and personal standards of responsibility.
(i) How important is it to be an individual?

(3) *Personal behaviour*

Standards of personal behaviour with reference to the following:
  exploitation of others;
  bullying;
  disobedience and rebellion against authority;
  jealousy and vindictiveness;
  shyness;
  facing adversity;
  fear and submissiveness;
  desire for security;
  conceit and possessiveness;
  greed;
  respect for others in family and circle of friends;
  codes of behaviour;
  are there changing standards and values?
  why people behave badly—insecurity, ignorance, fear, nervousness?
  good manners and courtesy;
  social responsibility in a community.

(4) *Personal and community health*

(a) Personal fitness and exercise—leisure pursuits, rest, posture.
(b) Personal discipline and responsibility.
(c) Personal hygiene and health habits—cleanliness and personal attraction.
(d) Food and diet: over and under-weight; cholesterol levels; food hygiene.
(e) Suitable clothing—fashion.
(f) Foot care and shoes.
(g) Dental health and fluoridation.
(h) Care of skin and hair; cosmetics.
(i) Care of eyes; colour blindness.
(j) Hearing—infections, impairments, aids, noise.
(k) Dirt and danger in smoking.
(l) Common illnesses and home nursing. Major diseases and community health—invalids, immunisation.
(m) Sexually transmitted diseases.

(n) Handicaps: mental and physical; attitudes; causes; effects; treatment; rehabilitation.
(o) Cancer education.
(p) Alcohol and drugs education.
(q) Road safety.
(r) Home safety: common accidents and their prevention.
(s) Safety in outdoor pursuits, including personal survival.
(t) Elementary first aid, including resuscitation (qualified instructor essential).
(u) Safety at work. Shops and Factory Acts.
(v) Parenthood.

(5) *Personal relationships*

(a) Need for affection, recognition, and acceptance.
(b) Self-understanding—knowing one's faults and limitations—developing personal potential and ways of coping with life.
(c) Need to live and co-operate with others. The words we use.
(d) How do we behave towards people we dislike and like?
(e) Loneliness in ourselves and others.
(f) Making friends—need to give as well as seek friendship.
(g) Recognising roles and attitudes, and the need to present oneself well to others.
(h) Boy/girl relationships. Sexual attraction; socially acceptable behaviour; courtship; recognition of courtesy and respect; exploitation and selfishness.

(6) *Friendship*

(a) What is a friend? What is an acquaintance?
(b) Discuss the meaning of true friendship—giving as well as taking. Self-understanding.
(c) What qualities do you expect in a friend?
(d) What qualities do you have which make you a good friend?
(e) Discuss changes in friendships of group members within the last five years. Why do these changes take place?
(f) Can we be attracted by someone we don't like? By someone we don't know?
(g) Discuss the differences of reaction to overtures of friendship between men and women.
(h) Friendships in groups, gangs and clubs: pressures to conform; status and role within groups.
(i) Friendships with the opposite sex: status symbol of dating; steady or casual relationships; friendship as part of marriage.

(7) *Relationships with others*

(a) What is a group? types of groups; the family group; the structure and functions of groups in the local community; the gregarious nature and inter-dependence of man; 'in' groups and 'out' groups; school groups.

(b) Unorganised groups: mass thinking and mob law; irrational behaviour in a crowd, gang bravado and panic in crowds, formation of public opinion.

(c) Deviant groups: homosexuals; gypsies; minorities; 'not our sort'—our reactions; stereotyping.

(d) The handicapped and their needs.

(e) Class, racial and religious prejudices in relationships.

(8) Sexual relationships

(a) Sex education and human biology.

(b) Sexuality, attitudes and values. Sex kept in perspective.

(c) Sex roles. Parenthood.

(d) Chastity and promiscuity.

(e) Infatuation, love and affection.

(f) Loving someone and being in love with someone.

(g) Premarital intercourse.

(h) Pregnancy outside marriage.

(i) Homosexuality.

(j) Contraception and abortion.

(k) Sexually transmitted diseases.

(l) Sexual behaviour and courtesy; mutual respect; exploitation and selfishness.

(m) The effect of alcohol, group pressures and drugs on behaviour.

(9) Family life

(a) Growing up in the family; the importance of play for pre-school children: the family socialises children; the family as a sheltered environment.

(b) Foster children; adopted children; only children; unwanted children.

(c) How do members of a family behave towards each other?

(d) What is family loyalty?

(e) Discuss family loyalty in large and small families.

(f) Make a list of causes of family friction.

(g) Bringing friends home.

(h) Parties.

(i) Parents' rules—understanding parents and representing their views.

(j) The family as a social institution; family trees; comparison of British family today with that of other cultures.

(k) Extended and nuclear families.

(l) Factors affecting marriage and the family partnerships, birth rate, family size.

(m) Age at marriage.

(n) Women at work.

(o) Differences between social classes, religious denominations and countries.

(p) Problem families.
(q) Communes
(r) The elderly.
(s) Are the traditional roles of men and women changing?
(t) School and home co-operation.
(u) Parentcraft.
(v) Home-making.

(10) *Marriage*

(a) Engagements. Liking same things (perhaps in a different way); looking at things in the same way; behaviour in the same things (morals, religion). People of different religions, morals, interests. Length of time to find out compatability.
(b) Anticipating the problems of marriage. Living with the same person for many years. Tolerance, sympathy, love, kindness, companionship— What other qualities would you expect of a partner?
(c) Teenage, mixed and arranged marriages. Ideals of love. Adolescent and adult viewpoints.
(d) Commitment and companionship.
(e) Rights and duties of wife and husband. Changing roles of men and women. Mothers at work.
(f) Home-making. Mortgages and hire-purchase. Family and personal budgeting. Pocket money.
(g) Divorce and separation. Living alone by choice.
(h) Parenthood; adoption; family planning.

(11) *Intolerance*

(a) Prejudice—how it is formed? Family background? Mass media? Stereo-typing?
(b) Sense of security of belonging to a group. Do we reject what is outside our group? 'Not our sort'. Often any person found doing wrong is associated with a group—is this fair? Class discrimination.
(c) Racial problems.
(d) Inter-racial marriages.
(e) Amicable relationships at school, work or leisure, with people having different views on politics and religion.
(f) Jealousy, hatred, conceit, bullying.

(12) *Leisure*

(a) What is leisure?
(b) The shorter working week.
(c) Constructive and destructive uses of leisure.
(d) Social obligations.
(e) Rest and relaxation.
(f) Boredom.

(g) Laziness.
(h) 'My time's my own'.
(i) Local leisure facilities.
(j) Changes in leisure activities.
(k) Leisure patterns in different social classes and in different occupations.
(l) Individual and shared leisure activities.
(m) Wasting time—has inactivity a positive value?
(n) How does use of leisure make work for others?
(o) Misuse—pornography, gambling, drunkenness.
(p) Voluntary work can: counteract tendency to passive acceptance of 'laid on' systems of service and entertinaments; give opportunity to co-operate and mix with others—mutual understanding; humanise public affairs; give experience in responsibility and administration.
(q) Future happiness compared with present satisfaction.

(13) *Work*

(a) The value of further education and training. The problem of friends who ignore this and in the early years earn more money. Ambition.
(b) Careers for girls and married women. Equal rights legislation.
(c) Interviews. Careers guidance. Self assessment.
(d) Problems of leaving home; problems of living at home.
(e) Health and accommodation problems. Loneliness.
(f) Working conditions of today and yesterday. Technological change and its consequences for the individual and society. Legislation protecting people at work. Rights and obligations at work.
(g) Getting on with people at work. Understanding work discipline.
(h) Trade unions and their relationships with individuals and with society; industrial relationships.
(i) Employers and their expectations and needs. Relationships with foremen and management. Contacts with local industries.
(j) Rewards of standards of work. Job satisfaction. Training.
(k) 'Only mugs work'. Is work a good thing in itself? Economic incentives alone produce neither willing workers not good craftsmanship.
(l) Unemployment. Social service schemes. Preparation for retirement programmes.
(m) The need for personal convictions and standards of one's own.

(14) *Authority*

(a) Imagine yourself in a position of authority. What difficulties might you encounter if you were: a head waiter; a foreman; an employer; a police sergeant?
(b) What is the basis of authority: within school or workplace; within home; within the community?
(c) Are self control, will power, and conscience, bases of authority?
(d) Why do authorities impose standards of behaviour?
(e) Young people and the Law. Age and legal status.

(f) Petty and organised crime; delinquency; vandalism. The Courts and probation. Violence—cause and effect. Prevention or punishment? The police—duties, powers, obligations. Cost of crime to the community.

(g) Registering a legal protest against authority: newspapers; Ombudsman; pressure groups; duties and rights. Race Relations Acts 1965 and 1968; Trade Descriptions Acts 1968 and 1972; The Sale of Goods Act 1980. Weights and Measures Act 1878 to 1963; Food and Drugs Act 1944 to 1970; Hire-Purchase Regulations. The Consumer Council. Citizens Advice Bureaux. Other consumer societies and groups.

(15) *Freedom and young people*

(a) How important is freedom? How is it related to responsibilities?

(b) Can there be real freedom without the existence of risks—accidents, disease, unhappiness?

(c) Choosing a career. What do we look for—security, prospects, money, service?

(d) When you start earning money, how does your home situation change?

(e) What prevents you being treated like an adult?

(f) Should you always be treated like an adult, and how much responsibility for this falls on you? The reasons for rules.

(g) Does 'becoming an adult' depend only on size and age?

(h) Discuss respect for other people and their ideas. Balance between 'my' freedom and 'their' freedom.

(i) Behaviour with older people, parents, opposite sex, one's own friends, colleagues.

(j) Changing standards and values. Does absence of manners denote immaturity?

(k) Why do people behave badly—insecurity, ignorance, fear, nervousness?

(l) Is freedom a privilege or a right?

(16) *Environmental control and community care*

(a) Pollution of the environment: its causes, effects and methods of control—air, water, food and living conditions.

(b) National Health Service and local health and welfare services.

(c) School Health Service. Links with local health and welfare services.

(d) Social services, both voluntary and statutory: voluntary organisations, voluntary social services work by young people.

(e) World health and welfare: WHO, FAO, UNESCO, UNICEF, Red Cross, Oxfam and other international organisations that deal with poverty and lack of education in developing countries. UN Charter.

(f) Awareness and development of critical faculties. Creating a good environment. The development of critical awareness. Exploitation and manipulation by the mass media; influence of film, radio, T.V. advertising, Press and literature. Straight and crooked thinking.

(g) Recent developments in eduation.

(h) The affluent society. What is affluence? The development and problems of affluence. Possessions or people? Poverty in an affluent society. Gambling. Charity.

(17) *Social environment*

(a) Population: fertility, adoption, abortion, birth control, morality, disease, diet, medicine.
(b) Responsibilities to society: cultivating responsible attitudes.
(c) Conservation of the environment: the individual's contribution as well as the efforts of authority and industry. Conflicting needs and demands.
(d) Disease: history; infectious and non-infectious; control; common vectors of infection. Health hazards both in kinds of disease and precautions against them. VD.
(e) Chemical substances used in medicine: purpose of drugs in medication, dangers of self-medication, misuse and abuse of drugs and the dangers arising.
(f) Addictive practices: alcohol; tobacco; cannabis; and the known addictive drugs. Gambling, physical and social effects. Social attitudes.
(g) What is a good neighbour? Samaritans; Marriage Guidance Councils; Alcoholics Anonymous; NSPCC; RSPCA.

(18) *The environment affects everyone*

(a) Man as a technologist and as a farmer.
(b) World demands for energy.
(c) General development of machines and transport.
(d) Individuals and the State.
(e) Conservation movements.
(f) Urban problems.
(g) Effects of pollution.
(h) The future evolution of humans.
(i) World problems: population, hunger, poverty, disease, housing, apathy.
(j) Immigration and emigration.
(k) Ideologies and religions.
(l) Nationalism and internationalism.
(m) The need for 'communities'.

(19) *Morality and human behaviour*

(a) Living in a society of 'plural values'.
(b) Why is there uncertainty? Overthrow of traditional values. Systems based on authority. Religious authority, authority of moral codes.
(c) What does it mean to be human? What are we for? Religious and non-religious views.
(d) How do we decide what behaviour is right? The importance of rationality.

(e) Can we agree on any marks of a morally educated man e.g. respect for other people translated into action (service)?

(f) Qualities men admire in others:
Love (*philia, eros, agape*)
patience
faithfulness
sacrifice
courage
faith
Qualities men do not admire in others:
hatred
prejudice
greed
revenge
sloth
cowardice

(g) Who should make the rules? Church? State?
(h) What do I hope to achieve?
(i) What does personal happiness mean?
(j) What moral codes do we follow?
(k) Is every human being vulnerable?
(l) Does every human being have problems?
(m) Need for recognition and acceptance by all.

(20) *Health education as a general theme*

(a) *Personal health*
Personal hygiene
Fitness exercise and rest
Personal appearance
Dental health
Internal working of the body
Care of feet, ears, hair, eyes
Nutrition
Standards of personal behaviour
Growth and development
Understanding ourselves
Decision-making
Personal values and attitudes
Responsibility

(b) *Community health*
Cancer education
Diseases
Obesity
Sexually transmitted diseases
Alcohol and Alcoholism
Drug-taking
Smoking
Health services and public health

Medicines and common illnesses
Handicapped people
First aid
The elderly
Mental health and stress
World health
Food hygiene
Noise
Multi-cultural aspects of health
(c) *Health and the environment*
Road safety
Safety in the home
Safety at work
Water safety
Conservation
Pollution
Law and order
Mass media and its effect
Consumer education
Leisure
(d) *Family life and personal relationships*
Feelings and needs of other people
Tolerance
Friendship
Anxiety and stress
Preparation for marriage
Family life
Care of young children
Sexual relationships
Birth control and abortion
Work and leisure
Reproduction and birth
Home-making

Appendix G Reprinted by kind permission of
Lancashire Local Education Authority.

Appendix H

Curriculum 11–16: Health education in the secondary school curriculum

A working paper by the Health Education Committee of HM Inspectorate, December 1978

Introduction

All societies provide health education for their members. Attitudes to health are part of the value system of any society. They are developed in numerous subtle ways by the family, by peer groups, by clubs, societies and religious organisations, by the schools, by the publicity media, by the provision and siting of health and social services, by laws and their enforcement and by the behaviour of people who are emulated.

These attitudes need to be considered, discussed and evaluated within the school curriculum. Health is not a Utopian concept, but an important part of the ability to function and to adapt positively within the real world. The knowledge, skills and attitudes which contribute to it are necessary for everyone and need to be acquired before leaving school.

The importance of health education
(with reference to the main curriculum 11–16 papers)

Health education is part of *the education of the individual*. It should provide enough knowledge and understanding to afford people a reasonable chance of leading healthy, responsible and harmonious lives. It should contribute towards the making of decisions about behaviour in the light of changing knowledge and social patterns. In addition it should develop an individual's self esteem and ability to take responsibility for his own health.

It is relevant to a consideration of *education for family life and living in society* since:
(a) It is necessary to understand the effects behaviour may have on others, and to learn to adapt behaviour.
(b) Society provides health and welfare services and it is important to appreciate how these are provided and the social and economic advantages of the prevention of ill health

It is part of education *for the world of work*, for a worker who cannot maintain his own health and safeguard that of others is a liability. Each occupation carries its own hazards which need to be understood and guarded against by the employee as well as by the employer.

The components of health education

The essential content should include *knowledge* and consideration of:
(a) The structure of the human body, and its physical and emotional functions.
(b) Growth and development, physical and mental, through childhood into adult life.
(c) The needs of children and the roles of parents.
(d) Personal relationships of all kinds.
(e) The influence of social and environmental factors on personal and community health before and after birth (e.g. quality of housing; opportunities for leisure; drugs; alcohol; smoking; pollution).
(f) Prevention of accidents and the appropriate response should they occur.
(g) The changing patterns of disease.
(h) Social and medical services.
(i) Ethical and socio-political problems presented by new developments in medicine.
  The *attitudes* which health education seeks to develop include:
(a) A genuine belief and enjoyment in the attainment and maintenance of good health.
(b) The acceptance of responsibility for personal health.
(c) A sense of 'self-esteem' or 'self-worth'.
(d) Consideration for others and concern for the health of the individual, the family and the community.
  The *skills* which pupils need include:
(a) An understanding of their own characteristics and the way in which they themselves relate to and form relationships with other people.
(b) The ability to make responsible decisions affecting their own health and safety and those of others, based on a sound grasp of relevant facts and issues.
(c) The ability to interpret research and conclusions about health and safety in a way which can be understood and related to personal life-styles.
(d) The ability to analyse stress and potentially stressful situations, and to react positively to them.
(e) The ability to use social and medical services.

Health education in the school curriculum

The secondary school curriculum, including the 'hidden curriculum', provides a variety of opportunities for health education.

Health applications of work in traditional subjects

Most subjects can make a contribution to health education. When any teacher allows time for pupils to consider how physics or biology, RE or English literature, impinges on their own lives, their own behaviour or aspirations and how these may affect their own health or that of others, then this is health education. A traditional subject may become more interesting and more relevant to most young people when it is connected with their present or potential experience in this way. Biology and home economics lend themselves particularly well to this approach but all subjects benefit from this kind of motivation to some extent. When teaching sound in physics it is no great step to discuss deafness caused by noise in industry or pop groups, or deafness undetected in children leading to language delay and learning difficulties. History and geography provide opportunities for the discussion of the incidence of diseases and their control and of population problems. Mathematics can use the statistical evidence for correlation between various forms of behaviour and disease. It is on this sort of evidence that the public must decide whether or not to smoke, to support or reject fluoridation schemes, to walk to the station instead of driving. This knowledge is an essential basis for adult choices, yet how often are pupils given the opportunity to practise such decision making, or even to discuss the process?

Audiovisual resources, notably broadcasting, provide support for teachers wishing to broaden their curriculum by discussion of health topics.

Discussion relating to the real and immediate interests of young people is a necessary form of learning in health education, and the development of pupils' language will enhance the skills needed in a variety of inter-personal relationships.

This kind of health education assumes teachers are well-informed on health matters with the knowledge, the time and the sensitivity to emphasise positive health and prevention rather than malfunction and disease. But it would be foolish to rely on this form of health education without a serious attempt at co-ordination within each school or college.

Health education as an integral part of a planned curriculum

A number of schools provide a regular period in the timetable across one or more years for health related studies. The titles of these courses may vary but the contents are usually remarkably similar, consisting of six strands: physical, social and mental health, survival, use of services, and environmental education.

These components attempt to provide the basic facts which through the use of sensitive discussion techniques encourage the pupils to formulate attitudes and values for themselves, leading them to make decisions which will support and maintain healthy behaviour.

Not infrequently such courses have been formed from an amalgamation of Personal Relationships, Social Education, Careers and Health Studies, utilising the interests, enthusiasm and expertise of specialist teachers from several subject areas. Good co-ordination prevents unnecessary duplication and a planned programme develops which prevents the 'one-off' response to crisis situations.

Through dealing with sensitive and contentious issues teachers establish relationships with their charges which foster trust and empathy, besides creating strong links with supportive agencies outside the school which should persist into adult life.

Some local authorities, having identified some of our current problems as difficulties within personal relationships, provide a special training for teachers in aspects of personal development and methods of group discussion which provides opportunities for children to bring their personal problems to sympathetic and trained teachers or outsiders who act to some extent in a counselling role.

A few schools provide a systematic and objective health study either as a CSE course or within general studies in the sixth form. The Schools Council Humanities and Moral Education Projects, Schools Council Health Education Projects, the HEC Living Well Project. York General Studies, the BBC, ITV and others provide support for teachers who attempt new subject areas in this way.

Special courses of health education

Some schools may feel that they have not prepared their pupils adequately to cope with the obvious health problems and social or personal issues they may face. They may also feel that for several reasons the teachers cannot deal fully with some of the problems. If the essence of health education is response to change, the teachers may need up-dated information as well as the pupils. Moreover some of the topics may cause personal embarrassment, be too delicate and subject to the taboos of our particular society. The school may therefore feel that it needs outside help. A number of organisations outside the school are willing and able to provide this. Sometimes a school medical team may play a part and the Area Health Education Officer should be able to make suggestions and provide resources. However, preparation by the school itself and adequate follow-up are both essential and the LEA should be aware that these courses are taking place.

The 'hidden' curriculum

Attitudes and organisation within the school may well influence the attitudes that young people develop.

If the school provides physical activities which are purposeful and enjoyable for everyone, including some which can be carried over into adult life, it is acknowledging that exercise is desirable. Lack of exercise correlates strongly with some of the diseases of middle age.

If a school takes personal relationships seriously and not only discusses them within the curriculum but works to achieve good relationships between staff, between pupils and between staff and pupils, then there is some chance that young people will take these seriously in their working lives.

The attitude taken by the school to health inspections and health and welfare services may well influence the use of these in later years. With all our efforts to provide a welfare state, the inarticulate and the less well-to-do still do not make the best use of the services available.

If a school takes the trouble to make all pupils feel they matter and have a unique contribution to make to the community, it is lessening the chances that they will endanger their own health or that of others by indulging in practices which make them feel more adult but put them very much at risk from the health point of view. Self-esteem is a very important factor in regulating basic human drives and appetites.

The involvement of parents

'Health education is a part of the work of teachers which they share with parents to a greater degree than perhaps is apparent in other aspects of their job.' Parents welcome discussions on this issue. There is a growing interest in the schools in education for parenthood, including the importance of the home in providing basic health education.

Co-ordination

Health education is a continuing need for everyone but it must respond to changing and varying needs. It will therefore vary from time to time and from place to place. Each school will meet the perceived needs of its pupils in its own way; it is important that this response should be planned and co-ordinated, providing all pupils with an integrated and continuous programme carefully related to each stage of the personal development of both boys and girls.

References

1 *Prevention and health. Everybody's business.* DHSS 1976.
2 *Health Education in Schools.* DES, 1977.
3 Curriculum paper No. 14: *Health Education in Schools.* Scottish Education Department, 1974.
4 *Health Education in Secondary Schools.* Working Paper No. 57 Schools Council, 1976.
5 *Health Education Projects.* Schools Council and HEC, 1977.
6 *Health and Safety at Work.* TUC Guide. Congress House, March 1976.